LIFE IS FOR LIVING!

That's the message of this book. How many
people, knowing that they are in the wrong
job, the wrong environment, even the wrong
relationship, take that terrifying but
all-important step to break away, re-examine
themselves and their desires, and set out to
do what they want to do?

In *Your Erroneous Zones,* Dr. Wayne W.
Dyer, a top psychiatrist, tells how you can
learn to be yourself and live the way you
really want to live – whether it's dreaming by
the fireside or conquering mountains! He
explains how all those maddening little
personality hang-ups that lead to
dissatisfaction can be overcome and swept
away to leave the board clean for a new-look
you. If there are times when you're not happy
with yourself and your life, *Your Erroneous
Zones* may well provide the answer!

Your Erroneous Zones

DR. WAYNE W. DYER

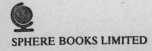

SPHERE BOOKS LIMITED

A SPHERE BOOK

First published in Great Britain simultaneously by Michael Joseph Ltd
(hardcover) and Sphere Books Ltd (paperback) 1977
Reprinted 1977, 1978 (twice), 1979 (three times), 1981 (twice), 1982, 1983
(twice), 1984 (twice), 1985, 1986 (twice), 1987, 1988, 1989, 1990 (twice)

Printed in England by Clays Ltd, St Ives plc

ISBN 0 7221 0565 7

Sphere Books Ltd
A Division of
Macdonald & Co (Publishers) Ltd
Orbit House, 1 New Fetter Lane, London EC4A 1AR
A member of Maxwell Macmillan Pergamon Publishing Corporation

TO
TRACY LYNN DYER
I Love You
in the special way
that I've written
about in these pages.

Contents

The whole theory of the universe is directed unerringly to one single individual—namely to You.

—WALT WHITMAN

Introduction—
A Personal
Statement

A speaker stood before a group of alcoholics determined to demonstrate to them, once and for all, that alcohol was an evil beyond compare. On the platform he had what appeared to be two identical containers of clear fluid. He announced that one contained pure water and the other was filled with undiluted alcohol. He placed a small worm in the container while everyone watched as it swam around and headed for the side of the glass, whereupon it simply crawled to the top of the glass. He then took the same worm and placed it in the container with alcohol. The worm disintegrated right before their eyes. "There," said the speaker. "What's the moral?" A voice from the rear of the room said quite clearly, "I see that if you drink alcohol, you'll never have worms."

This book has a lot of "worms" in it—meaning, you will hear and perceive exactly what you want to hear based upon many of your own values, beliefs, prejudices and personal history. Self-defeating behavior and the ways to overcome it are touchy areas to write about. Looking at yourself in depth with an eye toward changing might be something that you say you are interested in accomplishing, but your behavior often speaks otherwise. Change is tough. If you're like most people, every fiber of your being will resist having to take on the hard work of eliminating the thoughts that support your self-forfeiting feelings and behavior. But despite the "worms" I think you are going to like this book. I love it! And I loved writing it.

While I do not believe that mental health should be treated in a flip manner, neither do I support the notion that it must be a humorless enterprise, filled with arcane jargon. I have tried to avoid intricate explanations, largely because I do not believe that "being happy" is a complex affair.

Being healthy is a natural state, and the means for achieving it are within the grasp of each one of us. I believe that a judicious mixture of hard work, clear thinking, humor and self-confidence are the ingredients of effective living. I do not believe in fancy formulas, or historical excursions into your past to discover that you were "harshly toilet trained" and that someone else is responsible for your unhappiness.

This book outlines a pleasant approach to achieving happiness—an approach that relies on responsibility for and commitment to yourself, plus an appetite for living and a desire to be all that you choose to at this moment. It's an uncomplicated approach, a common sense approach. If you are a healthy, happy human being, you may find yourself thinking, "I could have written this book." You are right. You don't need a professional background in counseling and a doctorate in the helping professions to understand the principles of effective living. You don't learn them in a classroom or in a book. You learn them by being committed to your own happiness and by doing something about it. This is something I work on every day, while simultaneously helping others to make similar choices.

Each chapter of this book is written like a counseling session. This approach is aimed at providing as much opportunity for self-help as possible. A particular erroneous zone, or kind of self-destructive behavior, is explored, and the historical antecedents for the behavior in our culture (and therefore in you) are examined. The emphasis is on helping you understand *why* you are trapped in this self-defeating zone. Then specific behaviors that fall into this erroneous zone are detailed. The types of behavior we're talking about are everyday acts that may seem perfectly acceptable, but are, in reality, harmful to your own happiness. There are no examples from severe emotionally disturbed clinical cases, but rather the daily neurotic messages that we all send out. After a look at the behaviors in the erroneous zone we go on to an examination of the *reasons* for hanging on to behavior which does not make you happy. This entails a hard look at the psychological support system that you have erected to maintain self-defeating behavior, rather than giving it up. This section is an attempt to answer the questions, "What do I get out of my behavior?" and "Why does it persist if it is injurious to me?" As you examine each erroneous zone, you'll undoubtedly note that each of the "payoff" sections has similar messages. You'll discover that the reasons for keeping neurotic behavior are fairly consistent across all of the erroneous zones. Essentially it is safer to hang on to a learned response, even if it is self-destructive. Moreover, you can eliminate having to change and take responsibility if you keep the erroneous zones intact. These payoffs of safety and security will be evident throughout the book. You'll begin to see that your psychological maintenance system functions to keep blame off you and the opportunity for change at bay. The fact that you maintain many self-defeating behaviors for the same reason only makes total growth more approachable. Eliminate these reasons and you'll eradicate your erroneous zones.

Each chapter concludes with some straightforward strategies for eliminating self-nullifying behavior. This format is exactly what a counseling session is all about; that is, exploration of the difficulty and where it surfaces, a look at the self-defeating behavior, insight into the "Why" of the behavior and concrete strategies for eliminating the troublesome area.

Occasionally this approach may strike you as repetitious. That's a good sign—a sign of effective thinking. I have been a therapist for many years. I know that effective thinking—thinking which can alter self-destructive behavior—does not occur just because something is said. An insight must be repeated, and repeated, and repeated again. Only then, when it is fully accepted and understood, do you begin to alter behavior. It is for this reason that certain themes must be hammered at again and again in the pages of this book, just as they must be brought up again and again in successive counseling sessions.

There are two central themes that wind throughout the pages of this book. The first involves your ability to make choices about your own emotions. Begin to examine your life in the light of choices you have made or failed to make. This puts all responsibility for what you are and how you feel on you. Becoming happier and more effective will mean becoming more aware of the choices that are available to you. YOU ARE THE SUM TOTAL OF YOUR CHOICES, and I am just "far out" enough to believe that with an appropriate amount of motivation and effort you can be anything you choose.

The second theme that will be emphasized within these pages is that of taking charge of your present moments. This is a phrase that will reappear many times. It is an essential part of eliminating your erroneous zones and creating your happiness. There is only one moment in which you can experience anything, and that is now, yet a great deal of time is thrown away by dwelling on past or future experiences. Turning your now into total fulfillment is the touchstone of effective living, and virtually all self-defeating behaviors (erroneous zones) are efforts at living in a moment other than the current one.

Choice and present-moment living will be stressed on almost every page of this book. With a careful reading, you'll soon begin to ask yourself questions that have never occurred to you before. "Why am I choosing to feel upset right now?" and "How can I make more effective use of my present moments?" are the internal queries of a person moving away from erroneous zones toward self-reliance and happiness.

This book concludes with a brief portrait of a person who has eliminated all erroneous zones and is living in an internally rather than externally controlled emotional world. The following twenty-five questions are designed to measure your capacity to choose happiness and fulfillment. Go through the questions as objectively as possible and assess yourself and how you live your present moments. "Yes" responses indicate personal mastery and effective choice-making.

1. Do you believe that your mind is your own? (Chapter I)
2. Are you capable of controlling your own feelings? (Chapter I)
3. Are you motivated from within rather than from without? (Chapter VII)
4. Are you free from the need for approval? (Chapter III)
5. Do you set up your own rules of conduct for yourself? (Chapter VII)
6. Are you free from the desire for justice and fairness? (Chapter VIII)
7. Can you accept yourself and avoid complaining? (Chapter II)
8. Are you free from hero worship? (Chapter VIII)
9. Are you a doer rather than a critic? (Chapter IX)
10. Do you welcome the mysterious and the unknown? (Chapter VI)
11. Can you avoid describing yourself in absolute terms? (Chapter IV)
12. Can you love yourself at all times? (Chapter II)
13. Can you grow your own roots? (Chapter X)
14. Have you eliminated all dependency relationships? (Chapter X)
15. Have you eliminated all blame and fault-finding in your life? (Chapter VII)
16. Are you free from ever feeling guilty? (Chapter V)

17. Are you able to avoid worrying about the future? (Chapter V)
18. Can you give and receive love? (Chapter II)
19. Can you avoid immobilizing anger in your life? (Chapter XI)
20. Have you eliminated procrastination as a life-style? (Chapter IX)
21. Have you learned to fail effectively? (Chapter VI)
22. Can you enjoy spontaneously without having a plan? (Chapter VI)
23. Can you appreciate and create humor? (Chapter XI)
24. Are you treated by others the way you want to be? (Chapter X)
25. Are you motivated by your potential for growth, rather than a need to repair your deficiencies? (Chapter I)

At any given moment of your life, you can choose to say yes to all of the questions above if you are willing to repeal many "shoulds" and "oughts" that you have learned throughout your life. The real choice is whether you decide to be personally free or remain chained to the expectations that others have of you.

A friend of mine, Doris Warshay, after hearing one of my lectures, wrote a poem to me which she titled *New Directions*.

> I want to travel as far as I can go,
> I want to reach the joy that's in my soul,
> And change the limitations that I know,
> And feel my mind and spirit grow;
>
> I want to live, exist, "to be,"
> And hear the truths inside of me.

I trust this book will help you to eliminate any "worms" or blinders that may be keeping you from beautiful new experiences and to discover and choose your own new directions.

I
Taking Charge
of Yourself

The essence of greatness is the ability to choose personal fulfillment in circumstances where others choose madness.

Look over your shoulder. You will notice a constant companion. For want of a better name, call him *Your-Own-Death*. You can fear this visitor or use him for your personal gain. The choice is up to you.

With death so endless a proposition and life so breathtakingly brief, ask yourself, "Should I avoid doing the things I really want to do?" "Should I live my life as others want me to?" "Are *things* important to accumulate?" "Is putting it off the way to live?" Chances are your answers can be summed up in a few words: Live . . . Be You . . . Enjoy . . . Love.

You can fear your death, ineffectually, or you can use it to help you learn to live effectively. Listen to Tolstoy's Ivan Ilych as he awaits the great leveler, contemplating a past which was thoroughly dominated by others, a life in which he had given up control of himself in order to fit into a system.

"What if my whole life has been wrong?" It occurred to him that what had appeared perfectly impossible before, namely that he had not spent his life as he should have done, might after all be true. It occurred to him that his scarcely noticeable impulses, which he had immediately suppressed, might have been the real thing, and the rest false. And his professional duties and the whole arrangement of his life and of his family, and all his social and official interests, might all have been false. He tried to defend all those things to himself and suddenly felt the weakness of what he was defending. There was nothing to defend. . . .

The next time you are contemplating a decision in which you are debating whether or not to take charge of yourself, to make your own choice, ask yourself an important question, "How long am I going to be dead?" With that eternal perspective, you can now make your own choice and leave the worrying, the fears, the question of whether you can afford it and the guilt to those who are going to be alive forever.

If you don't begin taking these steps, you can anticipate living your entire life the way others say you must. Surely if your sojourn on earth is so brief, it ought at least to be pleasing to you. In a word, it's your life; do with it what *you* want.

Happiness and Your Own I.Q.

Taking charge of yourself involves putting to rest some very prevalent myths. At the top of the list is the notion that intelligence is measured by your ability to solve complex problems; to read, write and compute at certain levels; and to resolve abstract equations quickly. This vision of intelligence predicates formal education and bookish excellence as the true measures of self-fulfillment. It encourages a kind of intellectual snobbery that has brought with it some demoralizing results. We have come to believe that someone who has more educational merit badges, who is a whiz at some form of scholastic discipline (math, science, a huge vocabulary, a memory for superfluous facts, a fast reader) is "in-

telligent." Yet mental hospitals are clogged with pa
tients who have all of the properly lettered credentials—
as well as many who don't. A truer barometer of intelligence is an effective, happy life lived each day and
each present moment of every day.

If you are happy, if you live each moment for everything it's worth, then you are an intelligent person.
Problem solving is a useful adjunct to your happiness,
but if you know that given your inability to resolve a
particular concern you can still choose happiness for
yourself, or at a minimum refuse to choose unhappiness, then you are intelligent. You are intelligent because you have the ultimate weapon against the big
N.B.D. Yep—*Nervous Break Down*.

Perhaps you will be surprised to learn that there is
no such thing as a nervous breakdown. Nerves don't
break down. Cut someone open and look for the
broken nerves. They never show up. "Intelligent" people do not have N.B.D.'s because they are in charge
of themselves. They know how to choose happiness
over depression, because they know how to deal with
the *problems* of their lives. Notice I didn't say *solve*
the problems. Rather than measuring their intelligence
on their ability to *solve* the problem, they measure it
on their capacity for maintaining themselves as happy
and worthy, whether the problem gets solved or not.

You can begin to think of yourself as truly intelligent on the basis of how you choose to feel in the face
of trying circumstances. The life struggles are pretty
much the same for each of us. Everyone who is involved with other human beings in any social context
has similar difficulties. Disagreements, conflicts and
compromises are a part of what it means to be human.
Similarly, money, growing old, sickness, deaths, natural
disasters and accidents are all events which present
problems to virtually all human beings. But some people are able to make it, to avoid immobilizing dejection
and unhappiness despite such occurrences, while others
collapse, become inert or have an N.B.D. Those who

recognize problems as a human condition and don't measure happiness by an absence of problems are the most intelligent kind of humans we know; also, the most rare.

Learning to take total charge of yourself will involve a whole new thinking process, one which may prove difficult because too many forces in our society conspire against individual responsibility. You must trust in your own ability to feel emotionally whatever you choose to feel at any time in your life. This is a radical notion. You've probably grown up believing that you can't control your own emotions; that anger, fear and hate, as well as love, ecstasy and joy are things that happen to you. An individual doesn't control these things, he accepts them. When sorrowful events occur, you just naturally feel sorrow, and hope that some happy events will come along so that you can feel good very soon.

Choosing How You'll Feel

Feelings are not just emotions that happen to you. Feelings are reactions you choose to have. If you are in charge of your own emotions, you don't have to choose self-defeating reactions. Once you learn that you can feel what you choose to feel, you will be on the road to "intelligence"—a road where there are no by-paths that lead to N.B.D.'s. This road will be new because you'll see a given emotion as a choice rather than as a condition of life. This is the very heart and soul of personal freedom.

You can attack the myth of not being in charge of your emotions through logic. By using a simple syllogism (a formulation in logic, in which you have a major premise, a minor premise and a conclusion based upon the agreement between the two premises) you can begin the process of being in charge of yourself, both thinkingly and emotionally.

Logic—Syllogism

MAJOR PREMISE: Aristotle is a Man.
MINOR PREMISE: All men have facial hair.
CONCLUSION: ARISTOTLE HAS FACIAL HAIR.

Illogic—Syllogism

MAJOR PREMISE: Aristotle has facial hair.
MINOR PREMISE: All men have facial hair.
CONCLUSION: ARISTOTLE IS A MAN.

It is clear that you must be careful as you employ logic that your major and minor premises agree. In the second illustration, Aristotle could be an ape or a mole. Here is a logical exercise that can forever put to rest the notion that you cannot take charge of your own emotional world.

MAJOR PREMISE: I can control my thoughts.
MINOR PREMISE: My feelings come from my thoughts.
CONCLUSION: I can control my feelings.

Your major premise is clear. You have the power to think whatever you choose to allow into your head. If something just "pops" into your head (you choose to put it there, though you may not know why), you still have the power to make it go away, and therefore you still control your mental world. I can say to you, "Think of a pink antelope," and you can turn it green, or make it an aardvark, or simply think of something else if you so choose. You alone control what enters your head as a thought. If you don't believe this, just answer this question, "If you don't control your thoughts, who does?" Is it your spouse, or your boss, or your mama? And if *they* control what you think, then send them off for therapy and *you* will instantly get better. But you really know otherwise. You and only you control your thinking apparatus (other than under extreme kinds of brainwashing or conditioning experimentation settings which are not a part of your life). Your thoughts are your own, uniquely yours to keep, change, share, or contemplate. No one else can get inside your head and have your own thoughts as you experience them. You do indeed control your thoughts, and your brain is your own to use as you so determine.

Your minor premise is hardly debatable if you examine the research as well as your own common sense. You cannot have a feeling (emotion) without first having experienced a thought. Take away your brain and your ability to "feel" is wiped out. A feeling is a physical reaction to a thought. If you cry, or blush, or increase your heartbeat, or any of an interminable list of potential emotional reactions, you have first had a signal from your thinking center. Once your thinking center is damaged or short-circuited, you cannot experience emotional reactions. With certain kinds of lesions in the brain you cannot even experience physical pain, and your hand could literally fry on a stove burner with no sensation of pain. You know that you cannot bypass your think-center and experience any feelings in your body. Thus your minor premise is lodged in truth. Every feeling that you have was preceded by a thought, and without a brain you can have no feelings.

Your conclusion is also inescapable. If you control your thoughts, and your feelings come from your thoughts, then you are capable of controlling your own feelings. And you control your feelings by working on the thoughts that preceded them. Simply put, you believe that things or people make you unhappy, but this is not accurate. You make yourself unhappy because of the thoughts that you have about the people or things in your life. Becoming a free and healthy person involves learning to *think* differently. Once you can change your thoughts, your new feelings will begin to emerge, and you will have taken the first step on the road to your personal freedom.

To look at the syllogism in a more personal light, let's consider the case of Cal, a young executive who spends most of his time agonizing over the fact that his boss thinks he is stupid. Cal is very unhappy because his boss has a low opinion of him. But if Cal didn't know that his boss thought he was stupid, would he still be unhappy? Of course not. How could he be unhappy about something he didn't know. Therefore, what his boss thinks or doesn't think doesn't make him unhappy. What Cal thinks makes him unhappy. Moreover, Cal makes himself unhappy by convincing himself that what someone else thinks is more important than what he thinks.

This same logic applies to all events, things and persons' points of view. Someone's death does not make you unhappy; you cannot be unhappy until you learn of the death, so it's not the death but what you tell yourself about the event. Hurricanes aren't depressing by themselves; depression is uniquely human. If you are depressed about a hurricane, you are telling yourself some things that depress you. This is not to say that you should delude yourself into enjoying a hurricane, but ask yourself, "Why should I choose depression? Will it help me to be more effective in dealing with it?"

You have grown up in a culture which has taught you that you are not responsible for your feelings even though the syllogistic truth is that you always were. You've learned a host of sayings to defend yourself against the fact that you do control your feelings. Here is a brief list of such utterances that you have used over and over. Examine the message they send.

- "You hurt my feelings."
- "You make me feel bad."
- "I can't help the way I feel."
- "I just feel angry, don't ask me to explain it."
- "He makes me sick."
- "Heights scare me."
- "You're embarrassing me."
- "She really turns me on."
- "You made a fool of me in public."

The list is potentially endless. Each saying has a built-in message that you are not responsible for how you feel. Now rewrite the list so it is accurate, so it reflects the fact that you are in charge of how you feel and that your feelings come from the thoughts you have about anything.

• "I hurt my feelings because of the things I told myself about your reaction to me."
• "I made myself feel bad."
• "I can help the way I feel, but I've chosen to be upset."
• "I've decided to be angry, because I can usually manipulate others with my anger, since *they* think *I* control them."
• "I make myself sick."
• "I scare myself at high places."
• "I'm embarrassing myself."
• "I turn myself on whenever I'm near her."
• "I made myself feel foolish by taking your opinions of me more seriously than my own, and believing that others would do the same."

Perhaps you think that the items in List 1 are just figures of speech, and that they really don't mean very much, but are simply figures of speech that have become clichés in our culture. If this is your rationale, then ask yourself why the statements in List 2 did not evolve into clichés. The answer lies in our culture, which teaches the thinking of List 1, and discourages the logic of List 2.

The message is crystal clear. You are the person responsible for how you feel. You feel what you think, and you can learn to think differently about anything—if you decide to do so. Ask yourself if there is a sufficient payoff in being unhappy, down, or hurt. Then begin to examine, in depth, the kind of thoughts that are leading you to these debilitating feelings.

Learning Not To Be Unhappy: A Tough Assignment

It is not easy to think in new ways. You are accustomed to a certain set of thoughts and the debilitating thoughts that follow. It requires a great deal of work to unlearn all of the habits of thought you have assimilated until now. Happiness is easy, but learning not to be unhappy can be difficult.

Happiness is a natural condition of being a person. The evidence is plainly visible when you look at young children. What is tough is unlearning all of the "shoulds" and "oughts" that you've digested in the past. Taking charge of yourself begins with awareness. Catch yourself when you say things like, "He hurt my feelings." Remind yourself what you're doing at the moment you're doing it. New thinking requires awareness of the old thinking. You have become habituated in mental patterns that identify the causes of your feelings as outside of yourself. You have put in thousands of hours of reinforcement for such thinking, and you'll need to balance the scale with thousands of hours of new thinking, thinking that assumes responsibility for your own feelings. It is tough, damn tough; but so what? That certainly is no reason to avoid doing it.

Think back to the time you were learning to drive a stick shift automobile. You were faced with what seemed to be an insurmountable problem. Three pedals but only two feet to make them work. You first became aware of the complexity of the task. Let the clutch out slow, ooops too fast, jerky business, gas pedal down at the same rate as you release the clutch, right foot for the brake, but the clutch must go in, or you jerk again. A million mental signals: always thinking, using your brain. What do I do? *Awareness*, and then after thousands of trials, mistakes, new efforts, the day comes when you step into your car and drive away. No stalling, no jerking and *no thinking*. Driving a stick shift has become second nature, and how did you do it?

With great difficulty. Lots of present-moment thinking, reminding, working.

You know how to regulate your mind when it comes to accomplishing physical tasks, such as teaching your hands and feet to coordinate for driving. The process is less well-known but identical in the emotional world. You've learned the habits you now have by reinforcing them all of your life. You get unhappy, angry, hurt and frustrated automatically because you learned to think that way a long time ago. You have accepted your behavior and never worked at challenging it. But you can learn to not be unhappy, angry, hurt, or frustrated just as you learned to be all those self-defeating things.

For example, you've been taught that going to the dentist is a nasty experience, and one that is associated with pain. You've always felt that it is unpleasant and you even say things to yourself like, "I hate that drill." But these are all learned reactions. You could make the whole experience work for rather than against you by choosing to make it a pleasant, exciting procedure. You could, if you really decided to use your brain, make the sound of the drill signal a beautiful sexual experience and each time the brrrrrr sound appeared, you could train your mind to envision the most orgiastic moment of your life. You could think something different about what you used to call pain, and choose to feel something new and pleasurable. How much more exciting and fulfilling to take charge and master your own dental world environment than to hang on to the old images and just endure.

Perhaps you're skeptical. You may say something like, "I can think all I want, but I still get unhappy when he starts to drill." Think back to the stick shift. When did you *believe* that you could drive it? A thought becomes a belief when you've worked on it repeatedly, not when you simply try it once and use your initial inability as the rationale for giving up.

Taking charge of yourself involves more than simply

trying on new thoughts for size. It requires a determination to be happy and to challenge and destroy each and every thought that creates a self-immobilizing unhappiness in you.

Choice—Your Ultimate Freedom

If you still believe that you don't choose to be unhappy, try to imagine this course of events. Each time you become unhappy you are subjected to some treatment you find unpleasant. Perhaps you are locked in a room alone for long periods of time or, conversely, forced into a crowded elevator where you must stand for days. You may be deprived of all food or forced to eat some dish you find particularly distasteful. Or perhaps you will be tortured—physically tortured by others, rather than mentally tortured by yourself. Imagine that you were subjected to any one of these punishments until you made your unhappy feelings go away. How long do you think you would continue to hold on to them? Chances are you would take control rather quickly. So the issue is not whether you can take control of your feelings, but whether you will. What must you endure before you'll make such a choice? Some people choose to go insane rather than take control. Others merely give up and succumb to a life of misery because the dividend of pity received is greater than the reward of being happy.

The issue here is your own ability to choose happiness or at least not to choose unhappiness at any given moment of your life. A mind-blowing notion perhaps, but one that you should consider carefully before rejecting, since to discard it is to give up on yourself. To reject it is to believe that someone else instead of you is in charge of you. But choosing to be happy might seem easier than some things which daily confound your life.

Just as you are free to choose happiness over unhappiness, so in the myriad events of everyday life you are free to choose self-fulfilling behavior over self-defeating behavior. If you drive in this day and age, chances are you find yourself frequently stuck in traffic. Do you become angry, swear at other drivers, berate your passengers, take your feelings out on anyone and anything in range? Do you justify your behavior by saying that traffic always sends you into a snit, that you simply have no control in a traffic jam? If so, you are accustomed to thinking certain things about yourself and the way you act in traffic. But what if you decided to think something else? What if you chose to use your mind in a self-enhancing kind of way? It would take time but you could learn to talk to yourself in new ways, to become accustomed to new behavior which might include whistling, singing, turning on a tape recorder to write verbal letters, even timing yourself with thirty-second postponements of your anger. You have not learned to like the traffic but you have learned to practice, very slowly at first, new thoughts. You have decided not to be uncomfortable. You have chosen to substitute in slow, progressive steps healthy new feelings and habits for old self-defeating emotions.

You can choose to make any experience enjoyable and challenging. Dull parties and committee meetings are fertile territory for choosing new feelings. When you find yourself bored, you can make your mind work in exciting ways, by changing the subject with a key observation, or writing the first chapter of your novel, or working on new plans which will help you to avoid these settings in the future. Using your mind actively means assessing the people and events which give you the greatest difficulty and then deciding on new mental efforts to make them work for you. In a restaurant, if you typically get upset over poor service, think first of why you should not choose to be upset because someone or something is not going the way you would like it to go. You're too worthy to be upset by someone else, especially someone who is so unimportant in your life. Then devise strategies to change the setting, or leave, or whatever. But don't just get perturbed. Use your brain to work for you, and eventually you'll have the terrific habit of not being upset when things go wrong.

Choosing Health Over Illness

You can also choose to eliminate some physical sufferings which are not rooted in a known organic dysfunction. Some common physical ailments, which often do not have an origin in a physiological disorder, include headaches, backaches, ulcers, hypertension, rashes, skin eruptions, cramps, fleeting pains and the like.

I once had a client who swore she had a headache every morning for the past four years. Each morning at 6:45 she waited for it to arrive and then took her pain pills. She also kept each of her friends and co-workers informed of how much she was suffering. It was suggested to the client that she wanted the headaches, and had actually chosen them as a means of being noticed and as a means of receiving sympathy and pity. It was also suggested that she could learn not to want this for herself and to practice making the headaches shift from a point located centrally on her forehead to one on the side of her head. She was going to learn that she controlled the headache by making it move around. The first morning she awakened at 6:30 A.M., and lay in bed awaiting her headache. When it arrived she was able to *think* it to another place in her head. She had chosen something new for herself and ultimately she stopped choosing headaches completely.

There is a burgeoning amount of evidence to support the notion that people even choose things like tumors, influenza, arthritis, heart disease, "accidents" and many other infirmities, including cancer, which have always been considered something that just happens to people. In treating what have been labeled "terminally ill" patients, some researchers are beginning to believe that helping the patient not to want the disease, in any form, may be a means of ameliorating the internal killer. Some cultures treat pain in this way, taking complete power over the brain, and making self-control synonymous with *brain*-control.

The brain, which is composed of ten billion, billion working parts, has enough storage capacity to accept ten new facts every second. It has been conservatively estimated that the human brain can store an amount of information equivalent to one hundred trillion words, and that all of us use but a tiny fraction of this storage space. It is a powerful instrument you carry around with you wherever you go, and you might choose to put it to some fantastic uses which you've never even considered up until now. Keep that in mind as you go through the pages of this book and try to choose new ways of thinking.

Don't be too quick to call such control quackery. Most doctors have seen patients who have chosen a physical malady for which there is no known physiological cause. It's not uncommon for individuals to become mysteriously sick when confronted with some kind of difficult circumstance, or to avoid illness when being sick is simply "impossible" at that time, and so postpone the effects, perhaps the fever, until the big event is over, and then collapse.

I know of a case of a thirty-six-year-old man trapped in a horrible marriage. He decided on January 15th that he was leaving his wife on March 1st. On February 28th he developed a 104 degree fever and began vomiting uncontrollably. This became a recurring pattern; each time he built himself up, he got the flu, or an attack of indigestion. He was making a choice. It was easier to be sick than to face the guilt, fear, shame and the unknown that go with separation.

Listen to the advertisements we see and hear on television.

"I'm a stockbroker. . . . So you can imagine the tension and headaches I must have. I take this pill to make it go away." Message: You can't control how you feel if you work in certain kinds of jobs (teachers, executives, parents) so rely on something else to do it for you.

We are bombarded with messages like this every day. The implication is clear. We are helpless prisoners who must have someone or something else do things for us. NONSENSE. Only you can improve your lot or make yourself happy. It is up to you to take control of your own mind, and then practice feeling and behaving in the ways that you choose.

Avoiding Immobilization

As you consider your potential for choosing happiness, keep in mind the word *immobilization* as the indicator of negative emotions in your life. You might believe that anger, hostility, shyness and other similar feelings are worth having at times, and so you want to hang on to them. Your guide should be the extent to which you are in any way immobilized by the feeling.

Immobilization can range from total inaction to mild indecision and hesitancy. Does your anger keep you from saying, feeling, or doing something? If so, then you are immobilized. Does your shyness prevent you from meeting people you want to know? If so, you are immobilized and missing out on experiences that are rightfully yours. Is your hate and jealousy helping you to grow an ulcer or to raise your blood pressure? Does it keep you from working effectively on the job? Are you unable to sleep or make love because of a negative present-moment feeling? These are all signs of immobilization. *Immobilization:* A state, however mild or serious, in which you are not functioning at the level that you would like to. If feelings lead to such a state, you need to look no further for a reason to get rid of them.

Here is a brief checklist of some instances in which

you may be immobilized. They range from minor to major states of immobility.

You are immobilized when . . .

You can't talk lovingly to your spouse and children though you want to.

You can't work on a project that interests you.

You don't make love and would like to.

You sit in the house all day and brood.

You don't play golf, tennis, or other enjoyable activities, because of a leftover gnawing feeling.

You can't introduce yourself to someone who appeals to you.

You avoid talking to someone when you realize that a simple gesture would improve your relationship.

You can't sleep because something is bothering you.

Your anger keeps you from thinking clearly.

You say something abusive to someone that you love.

Your face is twitching, or you are so nervous that you don't function the way you would prefer.

Immobilization cuts a wide swath. Virtually all negative emotions result in some degree of self-immobility, and this alone is a solid reason for eliminating them entirely from your life. Perhaps you are thinking of occasions when a negative emotion has a payoff, such as yelling at a young child in an angry voice to emphasize that you do not want him to play in the street. If the angry voice is simply a device for emphasis and it works, then you've adopted a healthy strategy. However, if you yell at others not to make a point, but because you are internally upset, then you've immobilized yourself, and it's time to begin working at new choices that will help you to reach your goal of keeping your child out of the street without experiencing feelings that are hurtful to you. For more on anger and fuse-lengthening behavior, see Chapter XI.

The Importance of Living in the Present Moment

One way to combat immobilization, however slight, is to learn to live in the present moment. Present-moment living, getting in touch with your "now," is at the heart of effective living. When you think about it, there really is no other moment you can ever live. Now is all there is, and the future is just another present moment to live when it arrives. One thing is certain; you cannot live it until it does appear. The problem here, however, is that we live in a culture which de-emphasizes the now. Save for the future! Consider the consequences. Don't be a hedonist. Think of tomorrow. Plan for your retirement.

Avoiding the present moment is almost a disease in our culture, and we are continually being conditioned to sacrifice the present for the future. Carried to its logical conclusion, this attitude is not merely the avoidance of enjoyment in the now, but an evasion of happiness forever. When the future does arrive it becomes the present and we must use it to prepare for the future. Happiness is something for the morrow and therefore ever elusive.

The disease of present-moment avoidance assumes many forms. Here are four typical examples of such dodging behavior.

Ms. Sally Forth decides to go into the woods to soak up nature and get in touch with her present moments. While in the woods she lets her mind wander and focuses on all of the things that she should be doing back home. . . . The kids, the groceries, the house, the bills, is everything O.K.? At other times her mind flits forward to all of the things she'll have to do when she gets out of the woods. There goes the present, occupied by past and future events, and that rare opportunity for present-moment delight in that natural setting is lost.

Ms. Sandy Shore goes to the islands to enjoy herself,

and spends her entire vacation basking in the sun—not for the delight of feeling the sun on her body, but in anticipation of what her friends back home will say when she returns with a magnificent tan. Her mind is on a future moment, and when that future moment arrives, she'll bemoan not being able to be back at the beach sunning herself. If you think society doesn't contribute to this sort of attitude, consider the slogan of one sun lotion company, "They'll hate you more back home if you use this product."

Mr. Neil N. Prayer has a problem with impotence. When he is experiencing the present moment with his wife, his mind is off and running on some past or future event, and his present just slips away. When he finally manages to concentrate on the present and begins making love, he imagines her to be someone else, while she similarly fantasizes about her absent lover.

Mr. Ben Fishen is reading a textbook and working hard at staying with it. Suddenly he discovers that he has just read three pages and his mind was on a mental excursion. He wasn't absorbing a single idea. He was avoiding the material on those pages even while his eyes were focusing on each word. He was literally participating in the ritual of reading, while his present moments were being taken up by thinking about last night's movie or worrying about tomorrow's quiz.

The present moment, that elusive time which is always with you, can be most beautifully experienced if you allow yourself to get lost in it. Drink in all of every moment and tune out that past which is over and the future which will arrive in time. Seize the present moment as the only one you have. And remember, wishing, hoping and regretting are the most common and dangerous tactics for evading the present.

Frequently avoidance of the present leads to idealization of the future. At some miraculous moment in the future life will change, everything will fall into place, and you will find happiness. When you achieve that special event—a graduation, a wedding, a child, a promotion—then life will begin in earnest. More often than not when the event arrives it will be disappointing. It will never live up to what you had imagined. Think back to that first sexual experience. After all that waiting there were no Fourth of July orgasms, no grand mal seizures, but rather a quizzical wondering why everyone made such a big deal about it, and perhaps a feeling of Is that all there is?

Of course, when an event doesn't live up to your expectations you can get out of the depression by idealizing again. Don't let this vicious circle become your life-style. Interrupt it now with some strategic present-moment fulfillment.

Way back in 1903, Henry James gave this advice in *The Ambassadors:*

> "Live all you can; it's a mistake not to. It doesn't so much matter what you do in particular, so long as you have your life. If you haven't had that what *have* you had? . . . What one loses one loses, make no mistake about that. . . . The right time is *any* time that one is still so lucky as to have. . . . Live!"

As you look back on your life, much the way Tolstoy's Ivan Ilych did, you'll find that you seldom experience regret for anything that you've done. It is what you haven't done that will torment you. The message, therefore, is clear. Do it! Develop an appreciation for the present moment. Seize every second of your life and savor it. Value your present moments. Using them up in any self-defeating ways means you've lost them forever.

The theme of present-moment awareness appears on every page of this book. The people who know how to grab that present moment and maximize it are the people who have chosen a free, effective and fulfilling life. It is a choice each of us can make.

Growth vs. Imperfection as Motivators

In your quest to become as happy and fulfilled in your life as you choose to be, you can be motivated by two types of need. The more common form of motivation is called imperfection or deficiency motivation, while the healthier variety is labeled growth motivation.

If you place a rock under a microscope and observe it carefully, you note that it never changes. But, if you put a piece of coral under that same microscope, you'll detect that it is growing and changing. Conclusion: The coral is alive, the rock is dead. How do you distinguish between a flower that is alive and one that is dead? The one that is growing is alive. The only evidence of life is growth! This is also true in the psychological world. If you are growing, you are alive. If you are not growing then you might as well be dead.

You can be motivated out of a desire to grow rather than a need to repair your deficiencies. If you recognize that you can always grow, improve, become more and greater, that is enough. When you decide to be immobilized or to experience hurtful emotions, you've made a nongrowth decision. Growth motivation means using your life energy for greater happiness, rather than having to improve yourself because you've sinned or because you are in some way incomplete.

A corollary of choosing growth as motivation is personal mastery in every present moment of your life. Mastery means you are the decider of your fate; you are not a coper, or a striver, or someone who adjusts to the world. Rather you choose what your world will be for you. George Bernard Shaw expressed it in *Mrs. Warren's Profession:*

People are always blaming their circumstances for what they are. I don't believe in circumstances. The people who get on in this world are the people who get up and look for the circumstances they want, and if they can't find them, make them.

But remember what was said at the beginning of this chapter. Changing the way you think, or feel, or live is possible but never easy. Let's be hypothetical for a moment. If you were told, at point of gun, that within one year you would have to complete a difficult task, such as running a mile in four minutes and thirty seconds, or performing a perfect jackknife dive from the high board, and failure to do so would result in your execution, you would set out on a regimented schedule in which you would practice each and every day until your time came to deliver. You would be training your *mind* as well as your body because your mind tells your body what to do. You would practice, practice, practice, never yielding to the temptation to quit or slack off. And you would deliver, and consequently save your life.

This little fairy story is, of course, intended to make a point. No one expects to train his body overnight and yet too many of us expect our minds to respond with just such alacrity. When we are trying to learn new mental behavior we expect to try it once, and have it become a part of us instantaneously.

If you really want to be neurosis-free, self-fulfilled and in control of your own choices, if you really want to achieve present-moment happiness, you will need to apply the same kind of rigid application to the task of unlearning the self-defeating thinking you have learned up until now that you would give to the learning of any difficult enterprise.

In order to master this kind of fulfillment, you'll need to repeat endlessly that your mind really is your own and that you are capable of controlling your own feelings. The remainder of this book will be an effort to help you in your personal goals by having you begin precisely that repetition of such themes: you can choose, and your present moments are yours for the enjoying—if you decide to be in charge of you.

II

First Love

Self-worth cannot be verified by others. You are
worthy because you say it is so. If you depend on
others for your value it is other-worth.

You may have a social disease, one that will not go
away with a simple injection. You are quite possibly infected with the sepsis of low-esteem, and the only
known cure is a massive dose of self-love. But perhaps,
like many in our society, you've grown up with the
idea that loving yourself is wrong. Think of others, society tells us. Love thy neighbor, the church admon-
ishes. What nobody seems to remember is love thyself,
and yet that is precisely what you're going to have to
learn to do if you are to achieve present-moment
happiness.

You learned as a child that loving yourself, which
was a natural thing for you then, was akin to being
selfish and conceited. You learned to put others ahead
of you, to think of others first because that showed you
were a "good" person. You learned self-effacement and
were nurtured on instructions like "share your things
with your cousins." It didn't matter that they were your
treasures, your prized possessions, or that mommy or
daddy might not be sharing their big-people toys with
others. You may even have been told that you were to
"be seen and not heard" and that "you ought to know
your place."

Children just naturally think of themselves as beautiful and terribly important, but by adolescence society's messages have taken root. Self-doubt is in full bloom. And the reinforcements continue as the years pass. After all, you're not supposed to go around loving yourself. What will others think of you!

The hints are subtle and not malicious in intent, but they do keep the individual in line. From parents and immediate family members to schools, churches and friends, the child learns all those fine social amenities that are the hallmarks of the adult world. Kids never acted that way with each other, except to please older folks. Always say please and thank you, curtsy, stand up when an adult enters, ask permission to leave the table, tolerate the endless cheek pinching and head patting. The message was clear: adults are important; kids don't count. Others are significant; you are insignificant. Don't trust your own judgment was corollary number one, and there was a full cargo of reinforcers that came under the subheading of "politeness." These rules, disguised under the word *manners,* helped you to internalize the judgments of others at the expense of your own values. It's not surprising that those same question marks and self-denying definitions persist into adulthood. And how do these self-doubts get in the way? In the important area of loving others you may be having a difficult time. Giving love to others is directly related to how much love you have for yourself.

Love: A Suggested Definition

Love is a word that has as many definitions as there are people to define it. Try this one on for size. *The ability and willingness to allow those that you care for to be what they choose for themselves, without any insistence that they satisfy you.* This may be a workable definition, but the fact remains that so few are able to adopt it for themselves. How can you reach the point of being able to let others be what they choose without insisting they meet your expectations? Very simple. By loving yourself. By feeling that you are important, worthy and beautiful. Once you recognize just how good you are, you won't have to have others reinforce your value or values by making their behavior conform to your dictates. If you're secure in yourself, you neither want nor need others to be like you. For one thing, you're unique. For another, that would rob them of their own uniqueness, and what you love in them are just those traits that make them special and separate. It begins to fit. You get good at loving yourself, and suddenly you're able to love others, to give to others, and do for others by giving and doing for yourself first. Then there are no gimmicks to your giving. You're not doing it for the thanks or the payoffs but because of the genuine pleasure you get from being a helper or a lover.

If the you is someone unworthy, or unloved by you, then giving becomes impossible. How can you give love if you're worthless? What would your love be worth? And if you can't give love, neither can you receive it. After all what can the love be worth if it's bestowed on a worthless person. The entire business of being in love, giving and receiving, starts with a self that is totally loved.

Take Noah, a middle-aged man who claimed to love his wife and children dearly. To show his affections he bought them expensive gifts, took them on luxurious holidays, and was always careful when away on business trips to sign his letters "love." Yet Noah could never bring himself to tell his wife or children that he loved them. He had the same problem with his parents of whom he was tremendously fond. Noah wanted to say the words; they ran through his head repeatedly, yet every time he tried to say "I love you," he got all choked up.

In Noah's head the words "I love you" meant he was putting himself on the line. If he said "I love you," someone must answer "I love you, too, Noah." His statement of love must be met with an affirmation of his own self-worth. Saying those words was taking too much of a chance for Noah, for they might not be answered and then his entire value would be in question. If, on the other hand, Noah could start with the premise that he was lovable, he would experience no difficulty in the "I love you." If he didn't get the desired, "I love you, too, Noah," then he would see that as having nothing to do with his own self-worth, since that was intact before he ever started. Whether or not he was loved in return would be his wife's problem, or whomever Noah was loving at the moment. He might *want* the other person's love, but it would not be essential to his self-worth.

You can challenge all of your self-feelings in terms of your ability to love yourself. Remember, at no time, under no circumstance is self-hate healthier than self-love. Even if you have behaved in a way that you dislike, loathing yourself will only lead to immobilization and damage. Instead of hating yourself, develop positive feelings. Learn from the error, and resolve not to repeat it but don't associate it with your self-worth.

Here is the guts of both self- and other-directed love. Never confuse your self-worth (which is a given) with your behavior, or the behavior of others toward you. Once again, it isn't easy. The messages of society are overpowering. "You're a bad boy," rather than "You've behaved badly." "Mommy doesn't like you when you behave that way" as opposed to "Mommy doesn't like the way you behave." The conclusions that you may have adopted from these messages are, "She doesn't like me, I must be a nerd" instead of, "She doesn't like me. That's her decision, and while I don't like it, I'm still important." R. D. Laing's *Knots* sums up the process of internalizing others' thoughts and equating them with one's self-worth.

My mother loves me.
I feel good.
I feel good because she loves me.
My mother does not love me.

I feel bad.
I feel bad because she does not love me.
I am bad because I feel bad.
I feel bad because I am bad.
I am bad because she does not love me.
She does not love me because I am bad.*

The habits of thought of childhood are not easily out-grown. Your own self-image may still be based upon others' perceptions of you. While it is true that your original self-profiles were learned from the opinions of adults, it is not true that you must carry them around with you forever. Yes, it is tough to shed those old shackles and wipe clean those unhealed scars, but hanging on to them is even tougher when you consider the consequences. With mental practice you can make some self-loving choices that will amaze you.

Who are the folks who are good at loving? Are they self-demolishing in their behavior? Never. Do they put themselves down and hide in the corner? Not so. Getting good at giving and receiving love starts at home, with you, with a vow to end any low self-esteem behaviors that have become a way of life.

Tuning in to Self-Acceptance

First you must destroy the myth that you have one single self-concept, and that it is either positive or negative all of the time. You have many self-images, and they vary from moment to moment. If you were asked, "Do you like yourself?" you might be inclined to lump all of your negative self-thoughts together into a collective "No." Breaking down the areas of dislike into specifics will give you definite goals to work on.

You have feelings about yourself physically, intellectually, socially and emotionally. You have an opinion about your abilities in music, athletics, art, mechanical

* R. D. Laing, *Knots* (New York: Vintage Books, 1970), p. 9.

undertakings, writing and on and on. Your self-portraits are as numerous as your activities, and through all of these behaviors there is always YOU, the person that you either accept or reject. Your self-worth, that friendly ever-present shadow, your consultant for personal happiness and personal mastery, must be unrelated to your self-assessments. You exist. You are human. That is all you need. Your worth is determined by you, and with no need for an explanation to anyone. And your worthiness, a given, has nothing to do with your behavior and feelings. You may not like your behavior in a given instance, but that has nothing to do with your self-worth. You can choose to be worthy to yourself forever, and then get on with the task of working on your self-images.

Loving Your Body

It all begins with the physical you. Do you like your body? If you answered no, try breaking it down into its component parts. Make a list of the items that you find objectionable. Starting at the top: your hair, your forehead, eyes, eyelids, cheeks. Do you like your mouth, nose, teeth and neck? How about your arms, fingers, breasts and stomach? Make a long list. Include the innards as well. Your kidneys, spleen, arteries and femurs. Now go to the obscure ingredients that make up you. How about your Rolandic fissure, cochlea, pinna, adrenal glands and uvula? You've got to make a very long list to check yourself out thoroughly. You don't *have* a nice body; you are your body; and disliking it means not accepting yourself as a human being.

Perhaps you do have some physical attributes you dislike. If they are parts of your body which can be changed, make changing them one of your goals. If your stomach is too big or your hair the wrong color for you, you can see them as choices you made in an earlier present moment, and make new present-moment decisions about them. Those parts which you disapprove and which cannot be changed (legs too long, eyes too narrow, breasts too small or too large) can be viewed in a new light. Nothing is *too* anything, and long legs are no better or worse than hair or non-hair. What you have done is bought contemporary society's definition of beauty. Don't let others dictate what will be attractive to you. Decide to like the physical you and declare it as worthy and attractive to you, thereby rejecting the comparisons and opinions of others. You can decide what is pleasing and make nonacceptance of yourself a thing of the past.

You are a human being. Human beings have certain odors, make certain sounds and have certain growths of hair. But society and industry send out certain messages about the human physical condition. Be ashamed of these human characteristics, they say. Learn masking behavior—especially if you mask the real you with our product. Don't accept yourself; hide the real you.

You can't get through an hour of television without getting the message. The advertisements that bombard you daily tell you to be contemptuous of the way your mouth, underarms, feet, skin and even genitals smell. "Change to our product and feel real and natural again." As if the way you are is unnatural and you should go around sending out cosmetic odors in order to like yourself better. So you deodorize each orifice with the right smelling stuff, because you don't accept a part of yourself that exists in all human beings.

I know of a thirty-two-year-old man, Frank, who has learned to reject all of his bodily functions labeling them as disgusting and unmentionable. Frank is compulsively clean about his body to the point of being uncomfortable whenever he sweats, and he expects the same kind of starchy-clean behavior from his wife and children. He rushes for the shower to rid himself of any offensive odors after mowing the lawn or playing a set of tennis. Moreover, he cannot have sex unless both he and his wife shower before and after. He cannot tolerate his own normal body odors, nor can he live with anyone who is more accepting of himself. Frank sprays his bathroom, uses a multitude of cosmetic products to keep himself smelling good, and he is concerned about anyone else disliking him when he becomes human and begins smelling like one. Frank has learned to reject his natural body functions and odors. He has adopted attitudes that reflect personal self-rejection, by being either embarrassed or apologetic whenever he allows his body to be natural. But being human means having many natural odors, and the person who is working at self-love and self-acceptance is in no way offended by his natural self. In fact, if Frank were to be totally honest about himself, and wiped out the learned messages of self-rejection, he might even be able to admit to enjoying his own body and all of the glorious odors it is capable of producing. While he might not wish to share those odors with others, he would at least be able to accept them in himself, tell himself that he, in fact, likes them, and experience no shame around others.

Self-acceptance means liking the entire physical you, and eliminating those cultural impositions to be proper or to merely tolerate your body when it behaves other than in a cosmetic fashion. This doesn't mean you have to go around flaunting yourself, but it does mean that you can learn to take private pleasure in being you.

Many women have accepted the cultural dispatches and behave in ways that they are supposed to when it comes to their own bodies. Shave your legs and underarms, deodorize yourself everywhere, perfume your body with foreign odors, sterilize your mouth, make up your eyes, lips, cheeks, pad your bra, spray your genitals with the appropriate bouquet and falsify your fingernails. The implication is that there is something unpleasant about the natural you, the essentially human you, and only by becoming artificial can you become attractive. That's the saddest part, that the end product is a fraudulent you that takes the place of the natural self you carry around with you for most of your life. You are being encouraged to reject that beautiful you. That advertisers would encourage you to do this is understandable in light of profits to be made, but that you would buy the products is less easy to understand in view of the fact that you're choosing to throw away the real you. You can stop hiding the beautiful, natural you. Thus if you choose to use cosmetic aids of any kind, it will not be based on disliking what you are covering up, but for reasons of novelty or personal fulfillment. Being honest with yourself in this realm is not easy, and it takes time to learn to distinguish what pleases us from what the advertising business says should please us.

Choosing More Positive Self-Images

It is possible to make the same kind of choices with all of your self-images. You can choose to think of yourself as intelligent by applying your very own standards to yourself. In fact, the happier you make yourself, the more intelligent you are. If you are deficient in any areas such as algebra, spelling or writing, it is simply the natural result of choices you have been making up until now. Should you decide to devote enough practice time to any of these tasks, you would undoubtedly be more proficient in them. If your image of yourself is of someone who is not too intelligent, remember what we said about intelligence in Chapter I. If you underestimate yourself, it is because you have bought that notion, and you compare yourself to others on certain school-related variables.

It may surprise you to hear this, but you can choose to be as bright as you desire. Aptitude is really a function of time, rather than some inborn quality. One support for this belief can be found in the grade norms for standardized achievement tests. These norms demonstrate that scores achieved by the top students at one grade level are achieved by the majority of students at a later grade level. Further studies show that although most students eventually reach mastery on each learning task, some students achieve mastery much sooner than do others.* Yet the label "deficient" or even "retarded" is often attached to those who move more slowly toward absolute mastery of a skill. Listen to John Carroll as he talks on this point in his article, "A Model for School Learning," which appeared in *Teachers College Record*.

> Aptitude is the amount of time required by the learner to attain mastery of a learning task. Implicit in this formulation is the assumption that, given enough time, all students can conceivably attain mastery of a learning task.

With enough time and effort you could, if you so chose, master almost any academic skill. But you don't make that choice, for very good reasons. Why should you put that kind of present moment energy into solving obscure problems or learning something that doesn't interest you? Being happy, living effectively and loving are far greater goals. The point is that intelligence is not something that you inherited or had otherwise bestowed upon you. You are as smart as you choose to be. Not liking how smart you've chosen to be is mere self-contempt, which can lead only to injurious consequences in your own life.

The logic of being able to choose your self-pictures applies to all of the photographs of you that are lodged in your brain. You are as socially adept as you choose to be. If you dislike the way you behave socially, you can work at changing the behavior and not confusing it with your own self-worth. Similarly, your artistic, mechanical, athletic, musical and other abilities are largely the result of choices and should not be confused with your worthiness. (See Chapter IV for a full treatment of your self-descriptions and why you've chosen them for yourself.) In the same light, the preceding chapter made a case for your *emotional* life being the product of your own choices. Self-acceptance based up-

* Benjamin S. Bloom, et al., *Handbook on Formative and Summative Evaluation of Student Learning* (New York: McGraw-Hill, 1971).

on what you believe to be appropriate for you is something you can make a decision about now. Repairing those things that don't measure up can be a delightful undertaking, and there's no reason to choose to feel unworthy, just because there are things about yourself that you're going to improve.

Self-dislike can take many forms, and perhaps you engage in some putting-down-of-yourself behavior. Here is a brief list of some typically recurring behavior that falls into this category of the self-veto.

- Rejecting compliments directed at you. ("Oh, this old thing" . . . "I'm really not smart, just lucky I guess" . . .)
- Making up excuses for why you look nice. ("It's my hairdresser, she could make a toad look good" . . . "Believe me, it's the wardrobe that does it" . . . "Green is my color" . . .)
- Giving credit to others when it rightfully belongs to you. ("Thank God for Michael, without him I would be nothing" . . . "Marie did all the work, I just stood around and supervised" . . .)
- Using other-directed references when speaking. ("My husband says" . . . "My mother feels" . . . "George always tells me that" . . .)
- Having your opinions verified by others. ("Isn't that right, dear?" . . . "That's what I said, didn't I, Martha?" . . . "Just ask my husband, he'll tell you" . . .)
- Refusing to order something you want, not because you can't afford it (although this may be your stated reason) but because you don't feel that you're worth it.
- Not having orgasms.
- Not buying yourself something because you think you have to buy it for someone else, although sacrificing is not necessary; or not treating yourself to the things you would like to own, because you're not worth it.
- Avoiding indulgences such as flowers, wine or whatever, which you love because that would be wasteful.

- In a crowded room, someone yells out, "Hey, Stupid," and you turn around.
- Using pet names for yourself (and having others use them as well) that are really put-downs, including Dum-dum, Silly, Sweetie-pie or Baby (for an adult), Funny-face, Shorty, Fatty, or Baldy.
- A friend or lover gives you a gift of jewelry. The thought in your head goes something like this . . . "You must have a drawer full of jewelry at home for other girls."
- Someone tells you that you look good. The sentence in your head is, "You're practically blind or you must be trying to make me feel good."
- Someone takes you to a restaurant or theater. You think, "This is how it is in the beginning, but how long will it last once he finds out what kind of a person I really am?"
- A girlfriend accepts a date and you feel that she is going along just to be charitable.

I once worked with a young woman who was quite attractive and obviously múch sought after by men. Shirley insisted, however, that all her relationships ended badly and that, though she wanted desperately to marry, she had never had the opportunity. It came out in counseling that Shirley was ruining each of her relationships without realizing it. If a young man told her he cared for her or loved her, Shirley's head contradicted with "He's only saying that because he knows it's what I want to hear." Shirley was always searching for a sentence that would repudiate her worth. There was no self-love and so she rejected efforts by others to love her. She didn't believe that anyone could find her appealing. Why? Because she didn't believe that she was worth being loved in the first place, and so the interminable cycle of renunciation was her way of reinforcing her notions of her lack of worth.

While many of the items in the list above may appear to be petty, they nevertheless are tiny indicators of self-rejection. If you sacrifice or refuse to be extravagant with yourself, which often turns out to be choosing hamburger-helper over lamb chops, it is because you don't feel you're worth the better cut. Perhaps you've been taught that common courtesy calls for denial of a compliment or that you really aren't attractive. These are the lessons you've learned and the self-denying behavior is now second nature. There are numerous examples of self-repudiation behavior that surface in conversations and in everyday behavior. And each time you engage in any kind of a self-put-down, you reinforce that old bugaboo that others have laid on you and reduce your own opportunities for any kind of love in your life, be it self or other-directed love. Surely you are too worthy to go around putting yourself down.

Accepting Yourself Without Complaint

Self-love means accepting yourself as a worthy person because you choose to do so. Acceptance also means an absence of complaint. Fully functioning people never complain, and particularly they don't complain about the rocks being rough, or the sky being cloudy or the ice being too cold. Acceptance means no complaining, and happiness means no complaining about the things over which you can do nothing. Complaining is the refuge of those who have no self-reliance. Telling others about the things you dislike in yourself helps you to continue the dissatisfaction since they are almost always powerless to do anything about it except deny it and then you don't believe them. Just as complaining to others accomplishes nothing, so permitting others to abuse you with their own tote bags full of self-pity and misery helps no one. A simple question to ask will generally end this useless and unpleasant behavior. "Why are you telling me this?" or "Is there anything I can do to help you with this?" By asking yourself the same questions, you will begin to recognize your complaining behavior as ultimate folly. It is time spent in a wasteful manner, time which might be put to better use in practicing self-loving kinds of activities, such as silent self-praise, or helping someone else to achieve fulfillment.

There are two occasions when complaining is least appreciated in the world: (1) Whenever you tell someone else that you are tired. (2) Whenever you tell someone else that you don't feel well. If you are tired, you can exercise several options, but complaining to even one poor soul, let alone a loved one, is abusing that person. And it won't make you less tired. The same kind of logic applies to your "not feeling well."

Nothing is being said here about informing others of how you feel when they can help you in any small way. What is being challenged is complaining to others who can do nothing but endure the grumbling. Additionally, if you are truly working on self-love, and you are experiencing any pain or discomfort, you will want to work on this yourself, rather than choosing someone to lean on and have them share your burden.

Complaining about yourself is a useless activity, and one which keeps you from effectively living your life. It encourages self-pity and immobilizes you in your efforts at giving and receiving love. Morcover it reduces your opportunities for improved love relationships and increased social intercourse. While it may get you attention, the noticing will be done in a light that will clearly cast shadows on your own happiness.

Being able to accept yourself without complaint involves an understanding of both self-love and the complaining process, which are mutually exclusive terms. If you genuinely love you, then complaining to others who can do nothing for you becomes absurdly impossible to defend. And if you notice things in yourself (and others) that you dislike, rather than complaining you can actively set about taking the necessary corrective steps.

The next time you are at a social gathering of four or more couples, you can try this little exercise. Chronicle how much conversation is actually spent in complaining. From self to others, to events, prices, the weather, and on and on. Now, when the party is over and everyone has gone their separate ways, ask yourself, "How much of the complaining that went on tonight accomplished anything?". "Who really cares about all of the things that we bemoaned tonight?" Then, the next time you are about to complain keep the uselessness of that night in mind.

Self-Love vs. Conceit

You may be thinking that all of this talk about self-love involves a form of obnoxious behavior akin to egomania. Nothing could be further from the truth. Self-love has nothing to do with the sort of behavior characterized by telling everyone how wonderful you are. That's not self-love, but rather an attempt to win the attention and approval of others by chest-thumping behavior. It is just as neurotic as the behavior of the individual who is overloaded with self-contempt. Boastful behavior is motivated by others, by an attempt to gain their favor. It means the individual is evaluating himself on the basis of how others see him. If he were not, he would not feel the need to convince them. Self-love means you love yourself; it doesn't demand the love of others. There is no need to convince others. An internal acceptance is sufficient. It has nothing to do with the viewpoints of others.

The Rewards for Not Loving Yourself

Why would anyone choose not to love himself? Where is the advantage? The dividends, while they may be unhealthy, are nevertheless there for you to examine. And this is the core of learning to be an effective person—understanding why you behave in self-defeating ways. All behavior is caused, and the road to eliminating any self-destructive behavior is strewn with the potholes of misunderstanding your own motives. Once you comprehend the *why* of your self-malice and the maintenance system for retaining it, you can begin to attack the behaviors. Without the understanding of self, the old actions will continue to recur.

Why have you chosen to engage in self-denouncing ways, however slight they may seem to you? It may be that it is just plain easier to buy the stuff that others tell you than to think for yourself. But there are other dividends as well. If you choose to not love yourself and treat yourself as unimportant by placing other heads higher than your own, you will . . .

* Have a built-in excuse for why you can't get any love in your life, that is, you simply are not worth being loved back. The excuse is the neurotic payoff.
* Be able to avoid any and all risks that go with establishing love relationships with others, and thereby eliminate any possibility of ever being rejected or disapproved.
* Find that it is easier to stay the way you are. As long as you're not worthy there is just no point in trying to grow or to be better and happier, and your payoff is remaining the same.
* Gain a lot of pity, attention and even approval from others, which substitutes nicely for the risky business of getting involved in a love relationship. Thus the pity and attention are your self-defeating rewards.
* Have many convenient scapegoats to blame for your own misery. You can complain and thus you won't have to do anything about it yourself.
* Be able to use up your present moments with mini-depressions, and avoid behavior that would help you to be different. Your self-pity will serve as your escape route.
* Regress to being a good little boy or girl, calling upon the leftover responses of a child and therefore pleasing those "big-people" that you learned to regard as superior to you. Your regression is safer than risk.
* Be able to reinforce your leaning-on-others behavior by making them more significant than you make

yourself. A leaning post is a dividend even though you're hurt by it.

• Be unable to take charge of your own life and live it the way you choose, simply because you won't feel that you are worth the happiness you covet.

These are the components of your self-scorn maintenance system. They are the reasons you choose to hang on to the old thinking and behavior. It is just plain easier, that is, less risky, to put yourself down than to try to get up. But remember, the only evidence for life is growth, and so to refuse to grow into a self-loving person is a deathlike choice. Armed with these insights into your own behavior, you can begin to practice some mental and physical exercises to encourage the growth of your own self-love.

Some Easy-to-Master Self-Love Exercises

The practice of self-love begins with your mind. You must learn to control your thinking. This requires a lot of present-moment awareness at the times when you are behaving in self-condemnatory kinds of ways. If you can catch yourself as you are doing it, you can then begin to challenge the thought in back of your behavior.

You find that you have just said something like, "I'm really not that smart, I guess I was just lucky to get an A on that paper." The bell should go off in your head. "I just did it. I behaved in a self-loathing way. But I'm aware of it now, and the next time I'll stop myself from saying those things I've been saying all of my life." Your strategy is to correct yourself out loud with a statement such as, "I just said I was lucky, but luck really had nothing to do with it. I got the grade because I deserved it." One small step toward self-love, the step being a recognition of your present-moment put-down and a decision to act differently. Before you had a habit; now you have an awareness of wanting to be different, and you have made a choice to make it happen. It's just like learning to drive a stick shift. Eventually you'll have a new habit which will not require constant awareness. You'll soon be behaving in all kinds of self-adoring ways naturally.

With your mind now working for, rather than against you, exciting self-love activities are on the horizon. Here is a brief list of such behaviors to which you can add as you achieve a sense of self-esteem based upon your own worth.

• Select new responses to others' attempts to reach you with love or acceptance. Rather than instantly being skeptical of a loving gesture, accept them with a "thank you" or "I'm happy that you feel that way."

• If there is someone that you feel genuine love toward, say it right out front "I love you" and while you check out the reactions you receive in return, pat yourself on the back for taking the risk.

• In a restaurant, order something you really enjoy no matter what it costs. Give yourself a treat because you are worth it. Begin to select items that you would prefer in all situations, including the grocery store. Indulge yourself with a favorite product because you are worth it. Outlaw self-denial unless it is absolutely necessary—and it rarely is.

• After a tiring day and a large meal take a brief nap or a jog in the park even if you have too many things to do. It will help you to feel one hundred percent better.

• Join an organization, or sign up for an activity that you will enjoy. Perhaps you've been putting this off because you have so many responsibilities that you just don't have the time. By choosing to love yourself, and partaking of the slices of life that you want, those others that you serve will begin to learn some self-reliance of their own. And you will find yourself with an absence of resentment toward them. You will be serving them out of *choice*, rather than obligation.

• Eliminate jealousy by recognizing it is a put-down of yourself. By comparing yourself to some other person and imagining you are loved less, you make others more important than you. You are measuring your own merit in comparison to another. Remind yourself that (1) Someone can always choose another without having it be a reflection on you, and (2) whether or not you are chosen by any significant other is not the way you validate your own self-worth. If you make it that way, you are doomed to eternal self-doubt, because of the uncertainty of how a particular someone out there is going to feel at any precise moment of any given day. Should he/she choose another, that choice reflects only the other, not you. With practice at self-love, any circumstances in which you've previously found yourself to be jealous will be reversed. You'll believe so much in you that you won't need the love or approval of others to give you value.

• Your self-love activity might also include new ways of treating your body, such as selecting good nutritional foods, eliminating excess weight (which can be a health risk as well as an indication of self-rejection), taking regular walks or bicycle rides, choosing plenty of healthy exercise, getting outdoors to enjoy fresh air because it feels good, and in general keeping your body healthy and attractive. Provided *you* want to be healthy. Why? Because you are important and are going to treat yourself that way. Any total day spent cooped up or inactive in boring routine activities is a vote for self-enmity. Unless you actually prefer being cooped up, in which case you make that choice.

• Sexually, you can practice greater self-love. You can stand naked in front of a mirror and tell yourself how attractive you are. You can get in touch with your body. Explore yourself sensually, give yourself goosebumps of shivery pleasure. With others, you can also choose sexual fulfillment for you, rather than making your partner's pleasure more important than your own. Only by choosing gratification for yourself can you give pleasure. If you aren't happy, generally your partner is disappointed. Moreover, when you choose yourself, others are more able to choose happiness for themselves. You can slow down the whole process of sex, teaching your lover what you like with words and actions. You can choose orgasm for yourself. You can make yourself achieve the ultimate physical experience by believing that you are worth it, and then getting lost in the excitement of verifying it for you. Why? Because you are worth it!

• You can stop equating your performance in anything with your own self-worth. You may lose your job, or fail a given project. You may not like the way you performed this or that task. But that doesn't mean that you are without worth. You must know for yourself, that you are worth something regardless of your achievements. Without this knowledge, you will be persistently confusing yourself with your external activities. It is just as absurd to make your self-value depend upon some outside accomplishment as it is to tie it in with some external person's opinion of you. Once you eliminate this confusion, you will be able to set about all kinds of undertakings, and your final score—while it may be interesting to you—will in no way determine how valuable you are as a person.

These, and many like them, are the actions of those who love themselves. They may often challenge the lessons that you've learned as you've grown-down. At one time, you were the epitome of self-love. As a child, you knew instinctively that you were worthy.

Now look back at the questions in the introduction to this book.

• Can you accept yourself without complaint?
• Can you love yourself at all times?
• Can you give and receive love?

These are the issues that you can work on. Setting personal goals to be in love with the most beautiful, exciting, worthy person ever—you.

III

You Don't Need
Their Approval

Needing approval is tantamount to saying, "Your view of me is more important than my own opinion of myself."

You may be spending far too many of your present moments in efforts to win the approval of others, or in being concerned with some disapproval that you have encountered. If approval has become a *need* in your life, then you have some work to do. You can begin by understanding that approval-seeking is a desire rather than a necessity. We all enjoy applause, compliments and praise. It feels good when we are mentally stroked. Who would want to give this up? Well, there's no need to. Approval in itself is not unhealthy; in fact, adulation is deliciously pleasurable. Approval-seeking is an erroneous zone only when it becomes a need rather than a want.

If you want the approval, you are simply happy to have the endorsement of other people. But, if you need it, you are going to collapse if you don't get it. That's when the self-destructive forces move in. Similarly, when approval-seeking becomes a need, you give up a chunk of yourself to the "outside person" whose advocacy you must have. If they disapprove, then you are immobilized (even in a small way). In such a case, you have chosen to wear your self-worth on your sleeve for someone to rub or not rub as they see fit. You feel

58

good inside only if they decide to administer some praise to you.

The need for approval of another person is bad enough, but the real trouble comes with the need for the approval of everyone for every act. If you carry around such a need, then you are bound for a great deal of misery and frustration in your life. Moreover, you will be incorporating a wishy-washy non-person self-image that will result in the kind of self-rejection that was discussed in the previous chapter.

The *need* for approval must go! No question marks here. It must be eradicated from your life if you are to gain personal fulfillment. Such need is a psychological dead end, with absolutely no benefits accruing to you.

It is impossible to go through life without incurring a great deal of disapproval. It is the way of humanity, the dues you pay for your "aliveness," something that simply cannot be avoided. I once worked with a middle-aged man who fit into the classic approval-needing mentality. Ozzie had a set of beliefs on all controversial subjects, including abortion, birth control, war in the Middle East, Watergate, politics and everything else. Whenever he encountered scorn he came unglued. He spent a great deal of his energy in getting everyone to sanction him for everything that he said and did. He related an incident with his father-in-law, in which he stated that he firmly believed in mercy killing, and he noticed his father-in-law wrinkling his brow in censure. Instantly, almost reflexively, Ozzie modified his position. . . . "What I meant was, if someone is conscious and actually asks to be killed, then mercy killing is O.K." He noticed his listener was in agreement and Ozzie breathed a little easier. With his boss he also declared his belief in mercy killing, but here he received a vociferous disagreement. . . . "How can you even say such a thing? Don't you know that's playing God?" Ozzie could not tolerate such repudiation, he quickly shifted into a new stance. . . . "What I meant was, only in extreme cases, when a patient is declared legally dead, then it's all right to pull the plug." Finally, his boss acquiesced, and Ozzie was once more off the hook. With his brother he announced his position on mercy killing and he received an instant concurrence. . . . "Whew." That was easy for Ozzie, he didn't even have to change in order to get his brother to approve of him. All of these examples were provided by Ozzie as he related his normal way of interacting with others. Ozzie travels in his social circles with no mind of his own, and his need for commendation is so strong that he constantly shifts his position in order to be liked. There is no Ozzie, only the happenstance reactions of others which determine not only how Ozzie feels, but also what he thinks and says as well. Ozzie is whatever others want him to be.

When approval-seeking is a need, the possibilities for truth are all but wiped away. If you must be lauded, . and you send out those kinds of signals, then no one can deal with you straight. Nor can you state with confidence what it is that you think and feel at any present moment of your life. Your self is sacrificed to the opinions and predilections of others.

Politicians as a class are generally not trusted. Their need for approval is prodigious. Without it they are out of work. Therefore, they often seem to speak out of both sides of their mouths, saying this to please Group A, and that to win the approbation of Group B. There can be no truth when the speaker is shifty and moves around the issues with a skillful kind of maneuvering that is designed to please everyone. Behavior like this is easy to spot in politicians, but more difficult to see in ourselves. Perhaps you've "cooled it" in order to placate someone or you've found yourself agreeing with someone whose disfavor you fear. You knew you would be unhappy if you were censured, so you modified your behavior to avoid it.

It is tough to handle rebuking and easier to adopt behavior that will bring approval. But when you take this easy way, you're making others' opinions of you more important than your own self-assessments. It's a vicious trap—and a difficult one to escape in our society.

In order to escape the bear trap of approval-seeking, which gives others' opinions control over you, it is important to examine the factors that foster the approval-seeking need. Here is a brief excursion down the developmental path that leads to a great deal of approval-seeking behavior.

Historical Antecedents of the Need for Approval

The need for approval is based on a single assumption. "Don't trust yourself—check it out with someone else first." Our culture is one that reinforces approval-seeking behavior as a standard of life. Independent thinking is not only unconventional, it is the enemy of the very institutions that constitute the bulwark of our society. If you've grown up in this society, you've been tainted by this attribute. "Don't swear by yourself" is the essence of the need for tribute—and the backbone of our culture. Make someone else's opinion more important than your own, then if you don't get their approval, you have every reason to feel depressed, unworthy, or guilty, since they are more important than you.

The bestowal of approval can be a great manipulator. Your worth is lodged in others and if they refuse to dole out their approval, you've got nothing. You are without worth. And so it goes, the more flattery you need, the more you can be manipulated by others. Any steps in the direction of self-approval and independence of the good opinion of others are movements away from their control. As a result such healthy moves get labeled as selfish, uncaring, inconsiderate and the like, in an effort to keep you dependent. To understand this vicious circle of manipulation, consider the profusion of approval-seeking cultural messages, which began when you were a child, and which continue to bombard you today.

Early Family Approval-Seeking Messages

It is important to emphasize here that young children truly do need acceptance from significant adults (parents) in their formative years. But approval should not be contingent upon being proper, nor should a child have to get a parent's sanction for everything he says, thinks, feels, or does. Self-reliance can be taught in the crib, and approval-seeking ought not be confused with love-seeking as you read this section. In order to encourage freedom from the need for approval in an adult, it is helpful to give the child an abundance of approval from the very beginning. However, if a child grows up to feel that he cannot think or act without first securing the permission of a parent, then the neurotic seeds of self-doubt are early planted. Approval-seeking as a self-defeating need is mentioned here in terms of a child being conditioned to check it out with Mommy or Daddy, rather than in the very healthy sense of wanting the love and acceptance of a caring parent.

In most cases our culture teaches a child to rely on others rather than trusting his own judgment. Check out everything with Mommy or Daddy. "What do I eat?", "When?", "How much?" Ask Mommy. "Who can I play with?", "When?", "Where?" "It's your room, but you must keep it this way! Clothes on a hook, bed made, toys in the toybox, and so on."

Here's another set of exchanges to reinforce dependence and approval-seeking:

"You can wear anything you like."

"How do you like this, Mommy?"

"No, no honey! Stripes and polka dots don't go together! Go back and change either the blouse or the slacks so that they match."

One week later . . .

"What should I wear, Mommy?"

"I've told you, wear whatever you like. Why do you always ask me?"

Why indeed . . .

At the grocery store a cashier asks the child, "Would you like a piece of candy?" The child looks at her mom. "Would I like a piece of candy?" she asks. She has learned to check out everything with her parents, including whether she wants something or not. From playing, eating and sleeping to establishing friendships, and thinking, there are very few messages of self-reliance being thrown at young children in the family. It stems from the fundamental belief of Daddys and Mommys that they own their children. Rather than helping children to think for themselves, solve their own problems and develop trust in themselves, parents tend to treat children as possessions.

Kahlil Gibran speaks eloquently of children who are treated as possessions in *The Prophet.*

> Your children are not your children.
> They are the sons and daughters of Life's long-ing for itself.
> They come through you but not from you,
> And though they are with you yet they belong not to you.*

The results of this strategy are evident in every "de-pendent" child. Mommy becomes a referee, a constant breaker-upper of fights, someone to squeal to when a brother is misbehaving, someone who literally has to do all the child's thinking, feeling and behaving for him. Don't trust yourself to resolve your difficulties. Mommy or Daddy will do it for you. Don't rely on yourself to make the decisions you are capable of, check it out with someone else first.

Children resist being molded into approval-seekers. There are numerous examples of this in the lives of all who come into contact with young people. Count-less parents have related to me their own experiences in toilet training their children. They state that the child seems to know what it is that is being asked of him and

* Kahlil Gibran, *The Prophet* (New York: Alfred A. Knopf Pub-lisher), p. 17.

they are aware that the child has the capacity to physically control his sphincter muscles. Yet the child stubbornly, deliberately, refuses to comply. Here is the first real protest against needing a parent's approval. The internal messages are: "You can tell me what to eat, what to wear, who to play with, when to sleep, when to come in, where to put my toys, and even what to think. But I'll do this, when *I* am ready." The first successful protest against needing Mommy and Daddy's approval for everything.

As a child you wanted to think for yourself, to rely on yourself. If your Dad was helping you put on your coat when you were small, you said, "I can do it myself." But too often the message in return was "I'll do it for you. We don't have time to wait," or "You're too little." That spark of independence, that desire to be your own person, which was so alive in you as a child, was often dampened with rely on Mommy or Daddy. If you don't, we'll disapprove and when we disapprove of you, you must disapprove of yourself. The family unit nurtures, in the form of good intentions, dependence and the need for approval. Parents who don't want any harm to come to their children resolve to protect them from danger. The result, however, is the opposite of that intended, for without the ammunition of knowing how to rely on the self in times of strife (solving one's own disputes, dealing with insults, fighting for honor, earning one's own way), it is impossible to build an arsenal of independent behavior for a lifetime.

While you may not recall all of the approval-seeking messages that were telegraphed to you as a child, many of them most likely came at an early age. And while many of the check-it-out-with-Mommy-or-Daddy messages were important for your own safety and health, others were sent to teach you a critical concept—proper behavior, behavior that will win approval. That approval, which should have been a given, became contingent upon your pleasing someone else. The important point here is not that approval isn't important, but rather that it should be given to a child freely, not bestowed as a reward for proper conduct. A child should never be encouraged to confuse his own self-esteem with anyone else's approval.

Approval-Seeking Messages from School

When you left home and arrived in school, you entered an institution that is designed expressly to instill approval-seeking thinking and behavior. Ask permission to do everything. Never bank on your own judgment. Ask the teacher to go to the bathroom. Sit in a particular seat. Don't leave it under penalty of a demerit. Everything was geared toward other-control. Instead of learning to think you were being taught not to think for yourself. Fold your paper into sixteen squares, and don't write on the folds. Study chapters one and two tonight. Practice these words in spelling. Draw like this. Read that. You were taught to be obedient. And if in doubt, check it out with the teacher. If you should incur the teacher's, or worse yet, the principal's wrath, you were expected to feel guilty for months. Your report card was a message to your parents telling them how much approval you had won.

If you look at the philosophy of your school, which was quite likely written down under the pressure of an accreditation team visit, you will very likely see a statement worded something like this:

We, at Anywhere High School, believe in the full educational development of each student. The curriculum is arranged so as to meet the individual needs of every student in our school. We strive for, and promote the self-actualization and individual development of our student body . . . etc., etc. etc.

How many schools or teachers dare to put these words into action? Any student who begins to show signs of self-actualization and personal mastery is quickly put in his place. Students who are independent, full of self-love, not susceptible to guilt and worry, are systematically labeled troublemakers.

Schools are not good at dealing with kids who show signs of independent thinking. In too many schools approval-seeking is the way to success. The old clichés of teacher's pet and apple polishing are clichés for a reason. They exist—and work. If you gain the acclamation of the staff, behave in the ways that they dictate, study the curriculum that is laid out in front of you, you'll emerge successful. Albeit with a strong *need* for approval, since self-reliance has been discouraged at virtually every turn.

By the time a student reaches intermediate school he has usually learned the approval lesson. Asked by his counselor what he would like to take in high school, he responds with "I dunno, you tell me what I need." In high school he may have a difficult time making decisions about what to take, and will feel much more comfortable with the decisions that are made for him. In the classroom he'll learn not to question what he is told. He'll learn to write a theme properly and the correct interpretations of *Hamlet*. He will learn to write papers based not on his own judgment and opinions, but on quotes and references that will substantiate everything he says. If he doesn't learn these things he'll be punished with low grades—and the teacher's disapproval. And by the time he is ready to graduate, he'll find it difficult to make a decision for himself, because for twelve straight years he has been told how to think and what to think. He has been fed on a solid diet of check it out with the teacher, and now, on graduation day, he is unable to think for himself. So he covets approval, and learns that gaining the sanction of others is tantamount to being successful and happy.

At college the same pattern of indoctrination continues. Write two term papers, use the correct format, set your margins at 16 and 84, make sure it is typed, have an introduction—body—and conclusion, study these chapters. . . . The big assembly line. Conform, please your professors and you'll make it. Then a student finally gets into a seminar where the professor says: "This semester you can study whatever you want in your field of interest. I will help you in your selection and the pursuit of your interest, but it's your education, and you can do with it as you please. I will help you all that I can." Panic sets in. "But how many papers do we have to do?", "When are they due?", "Do you want it typed?", "What books should we read?", "How many examinations?", "What kind of questions?", "How long do our papers have to be?", "Where do we set the margins?", "Do I have to come to class every day?"

These are the questions of an approval-seeker and it's not the least bit surprising in view of the educational methods we've examined. The student has been trained to do it for someone else, to please the professor, and to measure up to someone else's standards. His queries are the end product of a system that demands approval-seeking for survival. He is terrified of thinking for himself. It is just easier and safer to do what someone else expects.

Approval-Seeking Messages from Other Institutions

We acquire approval-seeking symptoms from other sources as well. Certainly the church has been a big influence in this area. You must please Jehovah, or Jesus, or someone external to yourself. The leaders of the church have misconstrued the teachings of the great religious leaders and attempted to teach conformity by using fear of retribution as a weapon. Thus, a man behaves morally not because he believes it to be appropriate for him, but because God wants him to behave that way. If in doubt, consult the commandments rather than yourself and what you believe. Behave because someone has told you to and because you will be punished if you don't, not because you know it to be the right behavior for you. Organized religion appeals to your approval-seeking needs. It may produce the same behavior that you would have chosen, but you haven't chosen it freely.

Using yourself as a guide and not needing the approval of an outside force is the most religious experience you can have. It is a veritable religion of the self in which an individual determines his own behavior based upon his own conscience and the laws of his culture that work for him, rather than because someone has dictated how he *should* behave. A careful look at Jesus Christ will reveal an extremely self-actualized person, an individual who preached *self*-reliance, and was not afraid to incur disapproval. Yet many of his followers have twisted his teachings into a catechism of fear and self-hate. (See Chapter XII for a complete description of a self-actualized individual.)

The government is another example of an institution that uses approval-seeking as a motivator for conformity. "Don't trust yourself. You haven't got the skills and wherewithal to function alone. We'll take care of you. We'll withhold your taxes because you would spend them before your tax bill came due. We'll force you to join Social Security because you wouldn't be able to decide for yourself—or save for yourself. You don't have to think for yourself, we'll regulate your life for you." And so you see many examples of the government going beyond its responsibility of providing essential services and governing society.

There are more rules on the books than there are people to disobey them. If someone decided to enforce every rule that exists, you would find yourself in violation of the law hundreds of times a day. Someone has decided when you can shop, and that you shouldn't drink alcohol on certain days at certain times. There are rules against everything, including what you can wear at a given time in a given place, how you can enjoy sex, what you can say, and where you can walk. Fortunately, most of these rules are not enforced. Nevertheless, your rule-makers are often folks who insist that they know what is good for you, know it more conclusively than you do yourself.

Every day we are bombarded with hundreds of cultural messages that encourage us to seek approval. The songs that we hear each day are filled with lyrical messages of approval-seeking, particularly the best-selling "popular" songs of the past three decades. Those sweet harmless lyrics may be more damaging than you realize. Here is a brief list of titles that send out the signal that someone or something else is more important than you. Without the approval of that special someone, the "I" would collapse.

- "I can't live, if living is without you."
- "You make me so very happy."
- "You make me feel like a natural woman."
- "You're nobody till somebody cares."
- "It all depends on you."
- "You make me feel brand new."
- "As long as he needs me."
- "If you go away."
- "People who need people."
- "You are the sunshine of my life."
- "No one else can make me feel the colors that you bring."
- "Without you, I'm nothing."

Perhaps you can try an exercise the next time you find yourself listening to a song that sends out the communiqués of approval-seeking. Check for those lyrics which reflect the way you've been taught to feel, that is, that you can't make it if someone disapproves of you or lets you down. Rewrite the songs to fit a mind-set of personal mastery rather than approval-seeking. For example:

- I make myself feel like a natural woman; it has nothing to do with you.
- I chose to love you. I must have wanted to do it then, but now I've changed my mind.

• Peoplē who *need* people are the unluckiest people in the world. But people who *want love* and *enjoy* people are making themselves happy.

• I make myself so very happy because of the things I tell myself about you.

• I am the sunshine of my life, and having you in it makes it even brighter.

• I can stop loving you, but at this point I choose not to.

While they admittedly won't sell, you can at least make a start on redirecting the unconscious messages that you hear, and which reflect the way people in our culture have learned to believe. "Without you I'm nothing" must be translated to "Without me I'm nothing, but having you makes this present moment very nice."

Television commercials make a special appeal to your approval-seeking thinking. Many of these commercial skits are efforts by the manufacturer to manipulate you into buying their products, by reinforcing the notion that other peoples' beliefs are more important than your own.

Consider the following dialogue when friends are coming over to your house for an afternoon of bridge:

1st Friend (sniffing the air): "Fried fish last night, dear?" said in a very disapproving tone.

2nd Friend: "George still smoking a cigar, I see," in a similarly unaccepting tone.

You: Looking hurt, distraught—nay destroyed—because others are disapproving of the odors in your own house.

Psychological message: "What others think of you is much more important than what you think of yourself, therefore, if you don't please your friends you deserve to feel bad."

Consider also the following two skits and the message:

1. A waitress putting a bib around a customer's neck at a lobster party notices "ring around the collar." The

wife shrivels in shame at the thought of not receiving approval from a strange waitress.

2. A woman shrinks in fear as she contemplates how her friends will view her if she has baggy pantyhose. "I just couldn't stand it if they thought something bad about me. I must have their approval, so I'll buy this brand over that one."

3. The mouthwash, toothpaste, deodorants and special spray advertisements are filled with psychological messages that you must have approval, and the way to get it is to purchase this particular item. Why do advertisers stoop to such tactics? Because they work! They sell. They recognize that people are infected with the need for acceptance and they capitalize on this need by creating little sketches that send out the right messages.

There you have it, a culture that prizes and encourages approval-seeking. It is hardly surprising that you've found yourself placing too much emphasis on what others think. You've been conditioned to do so throughout your life, and even if your own family was conscious of the need to help you to promote self-reliance, the ancillary cultural factors worked against them. But you don't have to hang on to this approval-seeking behavior. Just as you work at eliminating the habit of self-put-down, so too can you eradicate this approval-seeking habit. Mark Twain, writing in *Puddinhead Wilson's Calendar*, gives a cogent description of how to break a habitual pattern such as approval-seeking. "Habit is habit, and not to be flung out of the window by any man, but coaxed downstairs a step at a time."

Coaxing Approval-Seeking Downstairs, a Step at a Time

Take a look at the way the world works. To put it succinctly, you can never please everyone. In fact, if you please fifty-percent of the people you are doing quite well. This is no secret. You know that at least half of the people in your world are going to disagree with at least half the things you say. If this is accurate (and you need only look at landslide elections to see that forty-four percent of the population still voted against the winner), then you will always have about a 50-50 chance of getting some disapproval whenever you express an opinion.

Armed with this knowledge, you can begin to look at disapproval in a new light. When someone disapproves of something you say, instead of being hurt, or instantly shifting your opinion to gain praise, you can remind yourself that you've just run into one of those folks in the fifty percent who don't agree with you. Knowing that you'll always get some disapproval for everything you feel, think, say or do is the way out of the tunnel of despair. Once you expect it, you won't be inclined to hurt yourself with it, and you'll simultaneously stop equating the repudiation of an idea or a feeling with the repudiation of you.

You can never escape disapproval, no matter how much you may want it to go away. For every opinion you have, there is a counterpart out there with exactly the opposite view. Abraham Lincoln talked about this in a conversation at the White House reported by Francis B. Carpenter:

> ... If I were to read, much less to answer all the attacks made on me, this shop might as well be closed for any other business. I do the very best I know how—the very best I can; and I mean to keep doing so until the end. If the end brings me out alright, what is said against me won't amount to anything. If the end brings me out wrong, ten angels swearing I was right would make no difference.*

* Francis B. Carpenter, *Six Months with Lincoln in the White House* (Watkins Glen, N.Y.: Century House).

Some Examples of Typical Approval-Seeking Behavior

Like self-rejection, approval-seeking encompasses a large category of self-defeating behaviors. Among the most common kinds of approval-seeking activities are those detailed below.

• Changing a position, or altering what you believe because someone shows signs of disapproval.

• Sugar-coating a statement to avoid the reaction of displeasure.

• Apple-polishing in order to make someone like you.

• Feeling depressed or anxious when someone disagrees with you.

• Feeling insulted or put-down when someone states a contrary sentiment to your own.

• Labeling someone a snob, or "stuck-up," which is just another way of saying "Pay more attention to me."

• Being excessively agreeable and head nodding, even when you don't agree at all with what is being said.

• Performing chores for someone and feeling resentful about not being able to say no.

• Being intimidated by a sharp salesperson and buying something you don't want ... Or ... Fearing taking it back because he won't like you.

• Eating a steak in a restaurant that is not cooked the way you ordered it, because the waiter won't like you if you send it back.

• Saying things you don't mean just to avoid being disliked.

• Spreading bad news about deaths, divorce, muggings and the like, and enjoying the feeling of being noticed.

• Getting permission to speak, or to make a purchase, or to do anything, from a significant other in your life, because you fear the displeasure of that person.

• Apologizing for yourself at every turn—the excessive "I'm sorry's" that are designed to have others forgive you, and approve of you all of the time.

• Behaving in *nonconforming* ways for the purpose of gaining attention, which is the same neurosis as conforming for the sake of external approval. Thus, wearing tennis shoes with your tuxedo, or eating a handful of mashed potatoes and wanting to be noticed is still approval-seeking.

• Being pathologically late for all occasions. Here you can't help but be seen and it is an approval-seeking device which gets everyone to pay attention. You may be doing it out of a need to be distinguished, and hence you are controlled by those doing the noticing.

• Trying to impress others with your knowledge of something that you know nothing about by "faking it."

• Begging for compliments by setting yourself up for approval, and then feeling bad when they don't come.

• Being unhappy about someone you respect having a contrary point of view, and expressing it to you.

Obviously, this list can go on forever. Approval-seeking is a cultural phenomenon that is readily observable in all corners of our globe. It is only distasteful when it becomes a need, which, of course, is tantamount to giving up the self, and placing responsibility for how you feel in the hands of others whose approbation is being sought.

The Dividends for Approval-Seeking

A look at the *why* of this self-defeating behavior will be useful in coming up with some strategies for eliminating approval-seeking needs. Below are some of the more common reasons—mostly neurotic in nature— for hanging on to approval-seeking. Payoffs for approval-seeking as a need include:

• Placing RESPONSIBILITY for your feelings on others. If you feel the way you do (lousy, hurt, depressed, etc.) because someone else didn't approve of you, then THEY, not you, are responsible for how you feel.

• If they are responsible for how you feel because of withholding their approval, then any CHANGE in you is also impossible, since it is their fault that you feel the way you do. Then they are also responsible for keeping you from being different. Thus approval-seeking helps you to avoid changing.

• As long as they are responsible and you can't change, you don't have to take any risks. Consequently, hanging on to approval-seeking as a way of life will help you to conveniently avoid any risk-taking activities in your life.

• Reinforcing a poor self-image and therefore encouraging self-pity and do-nothingism. If you are immune from the need for approval, you are immune from self-pity when you don't get it.

• Reinforcing the idea that others must take care of you, and therefore you can revert to the child in you and be coddled, protected—and manipulated.

• Blaming others for what you are feeling, thereby creating a scapegoating effect for everything you don't like in your life.

• Deluding yourself that you are liked by those others you've made more important than yourself and thus feeling outwardly comfortable even though there is a cauldron of discontent seething inside of you. As long as the others are more significant, then the outward appearance is more important.

• Taking solace in the fact that others notice you, which gives you something to boast about to other approval-seeking friends.

• Fitting into the culture which applauds such behavior and winning you the favor of the many.

These neurotic payoffs are strikingly similar to the rewards for self-hate. In fact, the theme of avoiding responsibility, change and risk is at the heart of all the self-destructive thinking and behavior described in this book. Without all of the fancy diagnostic language, it is just plain easier, more familiar and less risky to hang on to neurotic behaviors. Approval-seeking as a need is obviously no exception.

A Look at the Supreme Irony of Approval-Seeking Behavior

For a moment, engage in a little fantasy. Assume that you really wanted approval from everyone and that it was possible to obtain it. Further assume that this was a healthy goal. Now, with this in mind, what would be the best, most efficient way to obtain your end? Before answering, think of the one individual in your life that seems to get the most approval. What is this individual like? How does he behave? What is it about him that attracts everyone? You probably have someone in mind who is candid, direct and straightforward, independent of other people's opinions, and fulfilled. He probably has little or no time for approval-seeking. This is very likely a person who will tell it like it is, despite the consequences. Perhaps he finds tact and diplomacy less important than honesty. He is not a hurtful person, just an individual who has little time for the game-playing that goes with speaking delicately and being careful to say it just right to avoid hurting feelings.

Isn't that ironic! The people who seem to get the most approval in life are those who never seek it out, who have no desire for it, and who are not preoccupied with achieving it.

Here is a little fable which is applicable here, since happiness is an absence of approval-seeking as a need:

A big cat saw a little cat chasing its tail and asked, "Why are you chasing your tail so?" Said the kitten, "I have learned that the best thing for a cat is happiness, and that happiness is my tail. Therefore, I am chasing it: and when I catch it, I shall have happiness."

Said the old cat, "My son, I, too, have paid attention to the problems of the universe. I, too, have judged that happiness is in my tail. But, I have noticed that whenever I chase after it, it keeps running away from me, and when I go about my business, it just seems to come after me wherever I go." *

So, if you want all of that approval, it is ironic that the most effective way to get it is to not want it and to avoid chasing after it and to not demand it from everyone. By being in touch with yourself and using your positive self-image as a consultant, much more approval will come to you.

Of course you will never get approval from everyone for everything that you do, but when you see yourself as worthy you'll never be depressed when approval is withheld. Disapproval will be viewed by you as the natural consequence of living on this planet where people are individual in their perceptions.

Some Specific Strategies for Eliminating Approval-Seeking as a Need

In order to cut down on your own approval-seeking behavior, you will need to come in touch with your own neurotic rewards for the continuation of the behavior. Beyond just thinking new self-enhancing thoughts when you contact disapproval (which is the most effective strategy you can employ), here are some specific things you can work on to get yourself out of the approval-seeking bind.

• Label disapproval with new responses that begin

* C. L. James, "On Happiness," in *To See a World in a Grain of Sand*, by Caesar Johnson (Norwalk, Conn.: The C.R. Gibson Co., 1972).

with the word *you*. For example, you note that your father is not agreeing with you and is even getting angry. Rather than shifting or defending yourself, simply respond with, "You're getting upset, and you feel that I shouldn't think the way I do." This will keep you in touch with the fact that disapproval belongs to him, not you. The you strategy can be employed any time, and with amazing results if you master the technique. You'll have to fight temptation to start with "I," thereby putting yourself in the position of defending or modifying what you just said in order to gain acceptance.

• If you think someone else is trying to manipulate you by withholding approval, say so. Instead of turning wishy-washy for the purpose of reaping some approval benefits, you can say out loud, "Generally I would shift my position now in order to get you to like me, but I really believe in what I said, and you'll have to deal with your own feelings about it." Or, "I guess you'd like me to change what I just said." The act of labeling it will be helpful in keeping in touch with your own thinking and behavior.

• You can thank someone for providing you with data that will be helpful in your growth, even though it was something you didn't like. The act of thanking puts an end to any approval-seeking. Your husband says that you're acting shy and nervous and he doesn't like it. Rather than trying to please him, you simply thank him for pointing it out. The approval-seeking behavior is gone.

• You can actively seek disapproval and work on yourself to not be upset. Select someone who is bound to disagree and, flying in the face of the disapproval, maintain your position calmly. You'll get better at not being upset, and not having to alter your own views. You'll be telling yourself that you expect this "contrariness," that it's all right for them to be the way they are, and that it really has nothing to do with you. By going after disapproval, rather than avoiding it, you'll build up your repertoire of behavior for dealing effectively with it.

• You can practice ignoring disapproval and not paying any attention to those who attempt to manipulate you with their denunciation. A colleague of mine was giving a lecture to a large audience in Berlin and a member of the audience was obviously seething at certain comments. Finally, he could stand it no longer and he picked on a minor point the speaker was making and rattled off all kinds of abusive remarks in the form of questions. He was attempting to bait the speaker and to seduce him into a neurotic interchange. My colleague's response to his tirade was a simple "O.K.," and he went on with his talk. By ignoring the abuse, he proved that he wasn't going to evaluate himself on the basis of what someone else felt. The heckler, of course, stopped. Had the speaker not felt good about himself, he might have made someone else's disapproval more important than his own good opinion of himself, and thus been upset when it was withheld.

• You can break the connecting chain between what others think, say and do, and your own self-worth. Talk to yourself when you encounter disapproval. "This is her stuff. I expect her to behave that way. It has nothing to do with me." This approach will eliminate the self-hurt that you inflict when you connect someone else's feelings with your own thoughts.

• Ask yourself this important question when you acquire disapproval. If they agreed with me, would I be better off? The answer is obviously no. Whatever they think can have no effect on you unless you let it. Moreover, you'll most likely find that you are better liked by those important folks like a boss or loved one when you can disagree with them without worry.

• Accept the simple fact that many won't ever understand you, and that it is O.K. Conversely, you won't understand many people who are very close to you. You don't have to. It's all right for them to be different and the most fundamental understanding you can have is that you don't understand. Gustav Ischheiser makes the point clearly in the following lines from *Appearances and Realities:*

. . . . If people who do not understand each other at least understand that they do not understand each other, then they understand each other better than when, not understanding each other, they do not even understand that they do not understand each other.

• You can refuse to argue or try to convince anyone of the rightness of your stance, and simply believe it.

• Trust yourself when buying clothes or other personal items without first checking it out with someone whose opinion you value more than your own.

• Stop verifying your facts by having them substantiated by a spouse or someone else with sentences like, "Isn't that right, honey?" or "Didn't we, Ralph?" or "Just ask Marie, she'll tell you."

• Correct yourself out loud whenever you've behaved in an approval-seeking way, thereby becoming aware of this tendency and practicing new behaviors.

• Work at eliminating the numerous apologies that you make even when you aren't really sorry for what you've just said. All apologies are pleas for forgiveness, and requests for forgiveness are approval-seeking which takes the form of, "I know you wouldn't like me if I really meant what I just did, so please say that I'm still okay." Apologizing is a waste of time. If you need someone else to forgive you before you can feel better, then you are giving them control over your feelings. While you can resolve not to behave in certain ways again, and see some of your behavior as unfortunate, apologizing behavior is a sickness that invests control of one's feelings in another.

• In a conversation, you can clock the amount of time that you speak and compare it with the amount spoken by your partner and acquaintances. You can work at not being the one who speaks infrequently and only when asked to participate.

• You can observe at your next get-together how many more times you are interrupted, and whether you always condescend when you speak simultaneously with another member of the group. Your approval-seeking may take the form of timidity. You can devise strategies for speaking without being interrupted by labeling the behavior as it crops up in your social milieu.

• Chronicle how many declarative versus interrogative sentences you make. Do you ask questions, seek permission and approval, as opposed to making a statement? For example, the question, "Nice day, isn't it?" puts the other person into the problem-solving role, and you into the approval-seeking position. A simple, "Nice day" is a declaration, rather than an attempt to seek an answer. If you are always asking questions of others you are into approval-seeking in what may seem a petty area, but which is reflective of your lack of confidence in your own ability to take charge.

These are the beginning steps to eliminating approval-seeking as a need in your life. While you are not striving to wipe out all approval, you are working toward not being immobilized in any small way because you don't get the blandishments you covet. Applause is pleasant and approval is a delightful experience. What you seek is immunity from pain when you don't get the cheers. Just as the dieter does not test his mettle for losing weight on a full stomach, or the individual who is quitting smoking doesn't measure his resolve after just putting out a cigarette, you won't really test yourself in the absence of disapproval. You can vow until you're orange in the face that you can handle disfavor and that you are not going to demand tribute from everyone, but until you are faced with the circumstances of contention you won't know how you are doing. If you can eliminate this troublesome erroneous zone from your life, the rest will seem easy, because you have been conditioned to need approval from your first breath on this earth. It will require a great deal of practice, but it is worth every bit of effort you put into it. Immunity from despair in the face of disapproval is the ticket to a lifetime of delectable personal present-moment freedom.

IV
Breaking Free from
the Past

Only a ghost wallows around in his past, explaining
himself with self-descriptors based on a life lived
through. You are what you choose today, not what
you've chosen before.

Who are you? How do you describe yourself? To
answer these two questions, you will very likely have to
refer to your own history, to a past that has been lived
through, but to which you are undoubtedly tied, and
from which you find it difficult to escape. What are your
self-descriptors? Are they neat little labels that you
have accumulated over a lifetime? Do you have a
drawer full of self-definitions which you use on a regular
basis? They may include tags such as I'm nervous,
I'm shy, I'm lazy, I'm not musical, I'm clumsy, I'm
forgetful, and a whole catalog of additional I'ms that
you use. You probably have many positive I'ms such
as I'm loving, I'm good at bridge, I'm sweet, as well.
These will not be dealt with here since the purpose of
this chapter is to help you grow, rather than to applaud
you for the areas of your life where you are operating
effectively.

Self-descriptors are not in themselves inappropriate,
but they can be used in harmful ways. The very act of
labeling might be a specific deterrent to growth. It's easy
to use the label as justification for remaining the same.
Sören Kierkegaard wrote, "Once you label me, you

negate me." When the individual must live up to the label, the self ceases to exist. The same is true of self-labels. You could be negating yourself by identifying with your trademarks, rather than your own potential for growth.

All self-labels come out of an individual's history. But the past, as Carl Sandburg said in *Prairie*, "is a bucket of ashes."

Check yourself out on the extent to which you are chained to your past. All self-defeating "I'ms" are the result of the use of these four neurotic sentences:

(1) "That's me."
(2) "I've always been that way."
(3) "I can't help it."
(4) "That's my nature."

There they are in one little package. The connectors that keep you from growing, changing and making your life (from this instant on—which is all the life you have) new, exciting and heaped with present-moment fulfillment.

I know of a grandmother who, each Sunday when she has the family over for dinner, decides exactly how much each person will eat by deliberately portioning out plates to her own specifications. She gives each person two slices of meat, a spoonful of peas, a clump of potatoes, and on and on. When asked, "Why do you do that?" she responds with, "Oh, I've always been that way." Why? Because "That's just the way I am." Grandma's rationale for her behavior is her own label which comes from a past of always having behaved in that manner.

Some people will actually use all four sentences in one shot when confronted with their behavior. You might ask someone why he always gets upset when the subject of accidents arises and he is likely to respond, "Oh, that's just me, I've always been that way. I really can't help it, it's just my nature." Whew! All four at once, and each being used as an explanation for why he will never be different and never even consider changing.

Your I'ms which describe self-canceling behavior can be traced to something that you've learned in the past. And every time you use one of these four sentences you are really saying, "And I intend to continue being the way I've always been."

You can begin to unknot the ropes that link you to your past and eliminate the fruitless sentences which are spoken to keep you just as you've always been.

Here is a typical list of "I'ms" that may
be included in your own self-portrait.

I'm Shy	I'm a Lousy	I'm Fat
" Lazy	Cook	" Not Musical
" Timid	" a Poor	" Not Athletic
" Afraid	Speller	" Sloppy
" Clumsy	" Tired Easily	" Stubborn
" Anxious	" Sickly	" Immature
" Forgetful	" Gauche	" Meticulous
" Not Me-	" Accident	" Careless
chanical	Prone	" Vindictive
" Poor at	" Short Fused	" Irrespon-
Mathe-	" Hostile	sible
matics	" Solemn	" Nervous
" A Loner	" Apathetic	
" Frigid	" Bored	

You are probably in there several times, or perhaps you are conjuring up your own list. The point is not which labels you choose, but that you choose to label yourself at all. If you are genuinely satisfied with any of the I'ms, then let them be, but if you can admit to any of these or other I'ms getting in your way at times, it's time to make some changes. Let's begin with an understanding of the origins of the I'ms.

People want to label you, to pigeonhole you into neat little categories. It's easier that way. D. H. Law-

rence saw the folly of this labeling process in his poem
*What Is He?**

> What is he?
> —A man, of course.
> —Yes, but what does he do?
> —He lives and is a man.
> Oh quite! but he must work. He must have a job
> of some sort.
> —Why?
> Because obviously he's not one of the leisured
> classes.
> —I don't know. He has lots of leisure. And he
> makes quite beautiful chairs.
> There you are then! He's a cabinet maker.
> —No, no!
> Anyhow a carpenter and joiner.
> —Not at all.
> But you said so.
> —What did I say?
> That he made chairs, and was a joiner and
> carpenter.
> —I said he made chairs, but I did not say he was
> a carpenter.
> All right then, he's just an amateur?
> —Perhaps! Would you say a thrush was a profes-
> sional flautist, or just an amateur?
> I'd say it was just a bird.
> —And I say he is just a man.
> All right! You always did quibble.

How Those "I'ms" Got Started

The antecedents to your I'ms fall into two categories.
The first kind of labels come from other people. They
were pinned on you as a child and you carry them

around with you to this day. The other labels are the result of a choice you made to keep from having to do uncomfortable or difficult chores.

The first category is by far the most prevalent. Little Hope is in the second grade. She goes to her art class every day, full of delight about coloring and dabbling in paint. Her teacher tells her that she really isn't all that good, and she begins to stay away from it because she doesn't like disapproval. Before long, she has the beginning of an I'm. I'm not good at art. With enough avoidance behavior she reinforces this notion and, as an adult, when asked why she doesn't draw, she says, "Oh, I'm not good at it. I've always been that way." Most I'ms are leftovers, hangers-on from a time when you heard such sentences as: "He's kind of clumsy; his brother is good at athletics, but he's the studious one." Or, "You're just like me, I was never good at spelling either." Or, "Billy was always the shy one." Or, "She's just like her father; he couldn't carry a tune with a wheelbarrow." These are the birth rites to a lifetime of I'ms that never get challenged. They are simply accepted as a condition of life.

Have a conversation with the people in your life who you feel are most responsible for many of your I'ms. (Parents, long-time family friends, old teachers, grandparents, etc.) Ask them how they think you got to be the way you are and if you've always been that way. Tell them you are determined to change and see if they believe you are capable. You'll be surprised at their own interpretations and how they feel you can't be any different, since "You've always been that way."

The second category of I'ms originates in those convenient tags that you've learned to place on yourself in order to avoid distasteful activities. I have been working with a client who is forty-six years old, and wants very much to attend college, since he missed out on his opportunity because of World War Two. But Horace is threatened by the prospect of being in academic competition with young people right out of high school. Fear of failure and doubt about his intellectual capacities scare Horace. He looks at catalogs regularly, and with the help he receives in counseling he has taken the appropriate entrance examinations and arranged an interview with an admissions official at a local community college. But he still uses his I'ms to skirt the actual doing process. He justifies his inaction with, "I'm too old, I'm not smart enough, and I'm not really interested."

Horace uses his I'ms to avoid something he genuinely wants. A colleague of mine employs them to get out of tasks he doesn't enjoy. He avoids having to fix the doorbell, or the radio, or any unpleasant handyman activity by simply reminding his wife, "Now you know, dear, I'm just not mechanical." These kinds of I'ms are adaptive behaviors, but they are nevertheless delusional excuses. Instead of saying, "I find this kind of activity dull or uninteresting, and I choose not to work at it in my present moments (which is perfectly logical and healthy)" it becomes easier to simply haul out an I'm.

In these cases, the individuals are saying something about themselves. They are stating, "I am a finished product in this area, and I am never going to be any different." If you are a finished product, all tied up and put away, you have stopped growing, and while you may very well want to hang onto some I'ms you may find that others are simply limiting and self-destructive.

Below is a listing of some labels that are relics of the past. If any of them belong to you, you might like to change them. To stay exactly the way you are in any area is to make one of those deathlike decisions described in Chapter I. Keep in mind that this is not a discussion of the things that you just plain don't enjoy, but rather a look at behavior that keeps you from activities from which you might choose a great deal of pleasure and excitement.

Ten Typical "I'm" Categories and Their Neurotic Dividends

1. *I'm poor at math, spelling, reading, languages, etc.*
   This I'm guarantees that you won't put in the effort required to change. The academic I'm is designed to keep you from ever having to do the hard work involved in mastering subject matter that you have traditionally found difficult or boring. As long as you label yourself inept, you have a built-in reason to avoid tackling it.

2. *I'm lousy at some skill areas such as cooking, sports, crocheting, drawing, acting, etc.*
   This I'm assures that you won't have to do any of these things in the future and justifies any poor performance in the past. "I've always been that way; it's just my nature." This attitude reinforces your inertia and, more important, it helps you to hang on to the absurd notion that you shouldn't do anything if you don't do it really well. Thus, unless you're the world champion, avoidance is better than doing.

3. *I'm shy, reserved, temperamental, nervous, afraid, etc.*
   The call is to genetics for these I'ms. Rather than challenging them and the self-destructive thinking which supports them, you simply accept them as a confirmation of the way you've always been. Also, you can blame your parents, and use them as the reason for your current I'm. You make them the cause and don't have to work at being different. You choose this behavior as a way to avoid being assertive in situations which have always been troublesome for you. This is a leftover I'm from a childhood in which others had an inherent interest in having you believe that you were incapable of thinking for yourself. These are the personality I'ms. These self-definitions help you to avoid the tough business of being different from

what you've always been. You simply define your
personality with a convenient I'm and you can now
excuse all kinds of self-forfeiting behaviors as out
of your control. You negate the notion that you can
choose your own personality, and rely instead on
your genetic misfortune to explain away all of those
personality traits that you would like to disown.

4. *I'm clumsy, uncoordinated, etc.*

These I'ms that you learned as a child enable you
to avoid potential ridicule that might come your
way because you aren't as physically skilled as
others. Of course, your lack of skill comes from
a history of believing those I'ms and hence avoiding physical activity, rather than from some inherent defect. You get good at what you practice, not
what you shun. Keep your I'm and stay on the
sidelines watching and wishing, but pretending that
you really don't like that sort of thing.

5. *I'm unattractive, ugly, big-boned, plain, too tall,
etc.*

These physiological I'ms are helpful in keeping you
from taking risks with the opposite sex, and in
justifying the poor self-image and lack of love
you've chosen for yourself. As long as you describe
yourself in this fashion, you have a ready-made
excuse for not putting yourself on the line in a
love relationship. And you don't have to work at
looking attractive to yourself, as well. You use your
mirror as justification for not taking a chance.
There's only one problem: we see exactly what we
choose to—even in mirrors.

6. *I'm unorganized, meticulous, sloppy, etc.*

These behavioral I'ms are convenient for manipulating others and in justifying why things have to
be done a certain way. I've always done it that way.
As if tradition were a reason to do anything. And
I'll always do it that way is the unstated message.
By relying upon the way you've always done it,
you don't ever have to entertain the risky notion of
doing it differently, and you can simultaneously

ensure that everyone around you will do it your way as well. This is the I'm that calls upon "policy" as a substitute for thinking.

7. *I'm forgetful, careless, irresponsible, apathetic, etc.*
These kinds of I'ms are especially useful to you when you want to vindicate yourself for some ineffective behavior. The I'm keeps you from ever going to work on your memory, or your carelessness, and you simply excuse yourself with your neat little, "That's me." As long as you can haul out this I'm when you behave in any of the ways described above, you will never have to work at changing. Just go on forgetting and reminding yourself that you can't really help it, and you'll always be forgetful.

8. *I'm Italian, German, Jewish, Irish, Black, Chinese, etc.*
These are your ethnic I'ms, and they work very well when you run out of other reasons to explain some behaviors that you have, which don't work for you, but are just too damned difficult to tackle. Whenever you find yourself behaving in stereotypical ways associated with your subculture, you simply trot out your ethnic I'm as a justification. I once asked a maître d' why he seemed so excitable and reacted to the slightest problem with outrageous outbursts. He responded, "What do you expect from me? I'm Italian. I can't help it."

9. *I'm bossy, pushy, authoritarian, etc.*
Here your I'm can allow you to continue hostile acts, rather than work at developing self-discipline. You varnish the behavior with "I can't help it, I've always been that way."

10. *I'm old, middle-aged, tired, etc.*
With this I'm you can use your age as a reason for not participating in what might be risky or threatening activities. Whenever you find yourself faced with an activity such as a sports event, dating after a divorce or the death of a spouse, traveling, or the like you can just say "I'm too old" and you will

have eliminated any attendant risks that go with trying something new and growth-producing. The implication of an "age-I'm" is that you are absolutely finished in this area, and since you will always get older, you are finished growing and experiencing anything new.

The "I'm" Circle

The rewards for hanging onto your past by trotting out your I'ms can be neatly summed up in the one word: avoidance. Whenever you want to dodge a certain kind of activity or to gloss over a personality defect, you can always justify yourself with an I'm. In fact, after you use these labels enough, you begin to believe them yourself, and at that present moment you are a finished product destined to remain as you are for the rest of your days. Labels enable you to avoid the hard work and the risk of trying to change. They perpetuate the behavior which has given rise to them. Thus, if a young man goes to a party with the belief that he is shy, he will behave as if he is shy and his behavior will further support his self-image. It's a vicious circle.

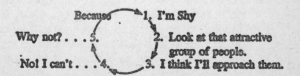

There you have it. Rather than intervening between point 3 and 4 on the circle, he simply exonerates his behavior with an I'm, and the attendant risk-taking that is necessary to get out of his trap is adroitly avoided. There may be many reasons for the young man's shyness, some of which probably go back to his childhood. Whatever the reasons for his fear he has decided not to go to work on his social-wariness, but to explain it away with a simple I'm. His fear of failing is strong enough to prevent him from trying. Were he to believe in the present moment and his ability to make a choice, his sentence would change from, "I'm shy," to "Up until now, I've behaved in a shy manner."

The vicious circle of shyness can be applied to virtually all I'ms that are self-diminishing. Consider the circle of a student who believes he's poor in math as he tackles his algebra homework.

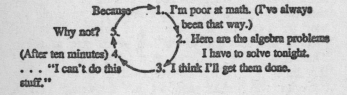

Because → 1. I'm poor at math. (I've always been that way.)

Why not? 5.

2. Here are the algebra problems I have to solve tonight.

(After ten minutes) 4.

... "I can't do this stuff."

3. I think I'll get them done.

Rather than stop between 3 and 4, and put in the extra time, consult a tutor, or struggle with it he simply stops. When asked why he flunked algebra class, he'll say "I've always been lousy in mathematics." Those infernal I'ms are the things that you call upon to exonerate yourself and to explain to others why you persist in a self-defeating pattern.

You can look at your own circle of neurotic logic and begin to challenge any aspect of your life in which you've chosen to be a finished product. The number one payoff for hanging onto your past and resting on your I'ms is avoidance of change. Every time you use an I'm to explain a behavior that you don't like, think of yourself in that gaily decorated box, all wrapped up as a finished package.

Certainly it is easier to describe yourself than to change. Perhaps you ascribe the reasons for your labels to your parents, or to other significant adults in your childhood such as your teachers, neighbors, grandparents and the like. By giving them responsibility for your present-day I'm you've given them a measure of control over your life today, elevated them to a higher position than you and ingeniously created an alibi for staying in your ineffective condition. A neat little payoff indeed, and one that provides you with a warranty against any risk-taking. If it's the "culture's" fault that you have this I'm, you can't do anything about it.

Some Strategies for Freeing Yourself from the Past and Eliminating Your Vexing I'ms

Leaving the past behind involves taking risks. You have become accustomed to your self-definitions. In many cases they function as a support system in your daily life. Some specific strategies for eliminating those I'ms include:

- Eliminating I'm wherever you can. Substitute with such sentences as, "Until today I've chosen to be that way," or "I used to label myself . . ."
- Announce to those close to you that you are going to work at eliminating some of your I'ms. Decide which are most important to eliminate and ask them to remind you whenever you haul them out.
- Set behavioral goals to act differently than you've ever done before. For example, if you consider yourself shy, introduce yourself to one person who you might otherwise have avoided.
- Talk with a trusted confidant who will help you combat the powers of the past. Ask him to signal you

silently with a tug to his ear each time he notices you
falling back into your I'm.

• Keep a journal on your self-destructive I'm behavior, and record your action as well as how you were
feeling about yourself while you were behaving that
way. For one week record in a notebook the exact
time, date and occasion when you used any of the self-
destructive I'ms, and work at diminishing the entries.
Use the list provided earlier in this chapter as a guide
to your journal-keeping.

• Watch out for the four neurotic sentences and
whenever you fall into using them, correct yourself *out
loud* in the following way. Change

"That's me." . . . to . . . "That was me."

"I can't help it." . . . to . . . "I can change that if
I work on it."

"I've always been that way." . . . to . . . "I'm going to
be different."

"That's my nature." . . . to . . . "That's what I used
to believe was my nature."

• Try to work each day on eliminating one I'm just
for that day. If you've used I'm forgetful as a self-
descriptor, devote Monday to working specifically at
being aware of this tendency, and see if you can alter
one or two forgetful behaviors. Similarly, if you don't
like your stubbornness I'm, give yourself one day to
be tolerant of contrary opinions, and see if you can rid
yourself of I'ms one day at a time.

• You can interrupt your own "I'm-Circle" between
point 3 and 4, and resolve to toss out those ancient
excuses for avoidance.

• Find something you've never done and set aside an
afternoon for that activity. After your three-hour immersion in a totally new activity, one that you've always
avoided in the past, see if you can still use the same
I'm that you applied that morning.

All of our I'ms are learned avoidance patterns, and
you can learn to be almost anything if you make the
choice to do so.

Some Final Thoughts

There is no such thing as human nature. The phrase itself is designed to pigeonhole people and to create excuses. You are the sum product of your choices, and every I'm you treasure could be relabeled, "I've chosen to be." Go back to the opening questions in this chapter, Who are you? and How do you describe yourself? Think about some delicious new labels that are in no way connected to the choices that others have made for you, or those that you've made until now. Those old tiresome labels may be keeping you from living your life as fully as you might.

Remember what Merlin said about learning:

"The best thing for being sad," replied Merlin, beginning to puff and blow, "is to learn something. That is the only thing that never fails. You may grow old and trembling in your anatomies, you may lie awake at night listening to the disorder of your veins, you may miss your only love, you may see the world about you devastated by evil lunatics, or know your honor trampled in the sewers of baser minds. There is only one thing for it then—to learn. Learn why the world wags and what wags it. That is the only thing which the mind can never exhaust, never alienate, never be tortured by, never fear or distrust, and never dream of regretting. Learning is the thing for you. Look at what a lot of things there are to learn—pure science, the only purity there is. You can learn astronomy in a lifetime, natural history in three, literature in six. And then, after you have exhausted a million lifetimes in biology and medicine and theocriticism and geography and history and economics, why, you can start to make a cartwheel out of the appropriate wood, or spend fifty years learning to begin to learn to beat your adversary at fencing.

After that you can start again on mathematics until it is time to learn to plough."*

Any I'm that keeps you from growing is a demon to be exorcised. If you must have an I'm, try this one on for size. "I'm an 'I'm' exorcist—and I like it."

* Terence H. White, *The Once and Future King* (New York: G. P. Putnam's Sons, 1958).

V

The Useless Emotions—
Guilt and Worry

> If you believe that feeling bad or worrying long
> enough will change a past or future event, then you
> are residing on another planet with a different reality
> system.

Throughout life, the two most futile emotions are guilt
for what has been done and worry about what might be
done. There they are! The great wastes—Worry and
Guilt—Guilt and Worry. As you examine these two
erroneous zones, you will begin to see how connected
they are; in fact they can be viewed as opposite ends
of the same zone.

X		Present		X
Guilt	(PAST)		(FUTURE)	Worry

There you have it. *Guilt* means that you use up your
present moments being immobilized as a result of *past*
behavior, while *worry* is the contrivance that keeps you
immobilized in the now about something in the *future*—
frequently something over which you have no control.
You can see this clearly if you try to think of yourself
as feeling guilty about an event that has yet to occur,
or to worry about something that has happened. Although one response is to the future and the other to the
past, they both serve the identical purpose of keeping

you upset or immobile in your present moment. Robert Jones Burdette wrote in *Golden Day:*

> It isn't the experience of today that drives men mad. It is the remorse for something that happened yesterday, and the dread of what tomorrow may disclose.

You see examples of guilt and worry everywhere, in virtually everyone you meet. The world is populated with folks who are either feeling horrible about something that they shouldn't have done or dismayed about things that might or might not happen. You are probably no exception. If you have large worry and guilt zones, they must be exterminated, spray-cleaned and sterilized forever. Wash out those little "w" and "g" bugs that infest so many sectors of your life.

Guilt and worry are perhaps the most common forms of distress in our culture. With guilt you focus on a past event, feel dejected or angry about something that you did or said, and use up your present moments being occupied with feelings over the past behavior. With worry, you use up those valuable nows, obsessing about a future event. Whether you're looking backward or forward, the result is the same. You're throwing away the present moment. Robert Burdette's *Golden Day* is really "today," and he sums up the folly of guilt and worry with these words.

> There are two days in the week about which and upon which I never worry. Two carefree days, kept sacredly free from fear and apprehension. One of these days is yesterday . . . and the other day I do not worry about is tomorrow.

A Closer Look at Guilt

Many of us have been subjected to a conspiracy of guilt in our lifetimes, an uncalculated plot to turn us into veritable guilt machines. The machine works like this. Someone sends out a message designed to remind you that you've been a bad person because of something you said or didn't say, felt or didn't feel, did or didn't do. You respond by feeling bad in your present moment. You are the guilt machine. A walking, talking, breathing contraption that responds with guilt whenever the appropriate fuel is poured into you. And you are well oiled if you've had a total immersion into our guilt-producing culture.

Why have you bought the worry and guilt messages that have been laid on you over the years? Largely because it is considered "bad" if you don't feel guilty, and "inhuman" not to worry. It all has to do with CARING. If you really *care* about anyone, or anything, then you show this concern by feeling guilty about the terrible things you've done, or by giving some visible evidence that you are concerned about their future. It is almost as if you have to demonstrate your neurosis in order to be labeled a caring person.

Guilt is the most useless of all erroneous zone behaviors. It is by far the greatest waste of emotional energy. Why? Because, by definition, you are feeling immobilized in the present over something that has *already* taken place, and no amount of guilt can ever change history.

DISTINGUISHING GUILT FROM LEARNING FROM YOUR PAST

Guilt is not merely a concern with the past; it is a present-moment immobilization about a past event. And the degree of immobilization can run from mild upset to severe depression. If you are simply learning from your past, and vowing to avoid the repetition of some specific behavior, this is not guilt. You experience guilt only when you are prevented from taking action now as a result of having behaved in a certain way previously. Learning from your mistakes is healthy and a necessary part of growth. Guilt is unhealthy because you are ineffectively using up your energy in the present feeling hurt, upset and depressed about a historical happening. And it's futile as well as unhealthy. No amount of guilt can ever undo anything.

The Origins of Guilt

There are two basic ways in which guilt becomes a part of the emotional makeup of an individual. In the first, guilt is learned at a very early age and remains with a grown-up as a leftover childish response. In the second case, guilt is self-imposed by an adult for an infraction of a code to which he professes to subscribe.

1. *Leftover Guilt*. This guilt is the emotional reaction which is carried around from childhood memories. There are scores of these guilt producers, and while they work in that they produce results in children, people still tote around these sentences as adults. Some of these leftovers involve admonitions like:

"Daddy won't like you if you do that again."

"You should feel *ashamed* of yourself." (As if that will be helpful to you.)

"Oh, all right, I'm only your mother."

As an adult, the implications behind these sentences can still produce hurt if a person disappoints his boss, or others whom he has made into parents. The persistent attempt to win their support is there, and so is the guilt when the efforts are unsuccessful.

Leftover guilt also surfaces in sex and marriage. It can be seen in the numerous self-reproaches and apologies for past behavior. These guilt reactions are present as a result of learning to be manipulated by adults in childhood, but they can still operate when the child has grown up.

2. *Self-imposed Guilt*. This second category of guilt reactions is a much more troublesome area. Here the individual is being immobilized by things he has done recently, but which are not necessarily tied to being a

child. This is the guilt imposed on the self when an
adult rule or moral code is broken. The individual may
feel bad for a long time even though the hurting can
do nothing to change what has happened. Typical self-
imposed guilt includes having told someone off, and
hating one's self for it, or being emotionally drained in
the present moment because of some act such as shop-
lifting, not going to church, or having said the wrong
thing in the past.

Thus you can look at all of your guilt either as
reactions to leftover imposed standards in which you
are still trying to please an absent authority figure, or
as the result of trying to live up to self-imposed standards which you really don't buy, but for some reason
pay lip service to. In either case, it is stupid, and, more
important, useless behavior. You can sit there forever,
lamenting about how bad you've been, feeling guilty
until your death, and not one tiny slice of that guilt
will do anything to rectify past behavior. It's over! Your
guilt is an attempt to change history, to wish that it
weren't so. But history is so and you can't do anything
about it.

You can begin to change your attitude about the
things over which you experience guilt. Our culture has
many strains of puritanical thinking which send out
messages like, "If it's fun, you're supposed to feel
guilty about it." Many of your own self-inflicted guilt
reactions can be traced to this kind of thinking. Perhaps
you've learned that you shouldn't indulge yourself, or
you mustn't enjoy a dirty joke, or you ought not to participate in a certain kind of sexual behavior. While the
restraining messages are omnipresent in our culture,
guilt about enjoying yourself is purely self-inflicted.

You can learn to savor pleasure without a sense of
guilt. You can learn to see yourself as someone who
is capable of doing anything that fits into your own
value system and does not harm others—and doing it
without guilt. If you do something, whatever it may be,
and you don't like it or yourself after having done it,
you can vow to eliminate such behavior for yourself in

the future. But to go through a self-inflicted guilt sentence is a neurotic trip that you can bypass. The guilt does not help. It not only keeps you immobilized, but it actually intensifies the chances that you'll repeat the unwanted behavior. Guilt can be its own reward as well as permission to repeat the behavior. As long as you retain the potential payoff of absolving yourself with guilt, you'll be able to keep yourself in that vicious treadmill that leads to nothing but present-moment unhappiness.

Typical Guilt-Producing Categories and Reactions

PARENTAL GUILT ON CHILDREN OF ALL AGES

Manipulating the child to complete a task through guilt:

Parent—"Donny, bring up the chairs from the basement. We'll be eating soon."

Child—"O.K., Mom, in a minute, I'm watching the ball game and I'll do it when this inning is over."

Parental guilt signal—"Never mind then, I'll do it —with my bad back. You just sit there and enjoy yourself."

Donny has visions of his mother falling down with six chairs landing on top of her. And he's responsible. The "I sacrificed for you" mentality is an exceedingly effective guilt producer. Here a parent can recall all of the hard times in which he gave up his happiness so that you might have something. You naturally ask yourself how you could be so selfish after you've been reminded of your debts. References to the suffering of childbirth are one example of this guilt-producing attitude. "I went through eighteen hours of labor just to bring you into the world." Another effective statement is, "I stayed married to your father because of you." This one is designed to make you feel guilty for Mama's bad marriage.

Guilt is an effective method for parental manipulation of a child's actions. "That's okay. We'll stay here by ourselves. You just enjoy yourself the way you've always done. Don't worry about us." Statements like this are effective in getting you to telephone or visit on a regular basis. With a slight twist you hear: "Whatsamatter; you got a broken finger and you can't dial a telephone?" The parent switches the guilt machine on and you behave accordingly, albeit resentfully.

The "You disgraced us" tactic is also useful. Or "What will the neighbors think?" External forces are marshaled to make you feel bad about what you've done, and to keep you from thinking for yourself. The "If you ever fail at anything you'll disgrace us" guilt excursion can make living with yourself after a shabby performance almost impossible.

Parental illness is a super guilt manufacturer. "You've made my blood pressure go up." References to "killing me" or "giving me a heart attack" are effective guilt producers, as well as blaming you for virtually all of the normal ailments associated with growing older. You need big shoulders to carry this guilt around, since it can literally last a lifetime, and if you are particularly vulnerable, you can even carry the guilt of a parent's death.

Sexual guilt imposed by parents is quite common. All sexual thought or behavior is fertile soil for the cultivation of guilt. "God forbid you should masturbate. It's bad." Through guilt you can be manipulated into the right sexual stance. "You should be ashamed for reading such magazines. You shouldn't even have such thoughts."

Socially appropriate behavior can be fostered with guilt. "How could you embarrass me by picking your nose in front of Grandma?" "You forgot to say thank you. Shame on you, do you want our friends to think I didn't teach you anything?" A child can be helped to learn socially acceptable behavior without the accom-

panying guilt. A simple reminder which follows an explanation of why the behavior is undesirable is much
more effective. For example, if Donny is told that his
constant interruptions are disconcerting and make conversation impossible, he will have the first seed planted
without having the guilt that goes with a statement
such as, "You're always interrupting, you should be
ashamed of yourself, it's impossible to talk with you
around."

Merely reaching adulthood does not put an end to
parental manipulation by guilt. I have a friend who is
fifty-two years old. He is a pediatrician of Jewish
extraction married to a non-Jewish woman. He keeps
his marriage a secret from his mother, because he is
afraid it might "kill her" or more aptly, he might kill
her. He maintains a separate apartment with all of the
household trimmings for the sole purpose of meeting
with his eighty-five-year-old mother every Sunday. She
does not know that he is married and owns his own
home where he lives six days a week. He plays this
little game out of fear and guilt about being married to
a "Shiksa." Although he is a fully grown man who
is highly successful in his own professional world, he
is still controlled by his mother. Each day he talks to
her from his office and lives out his bachelor fantasy.

Parental- and family-associated guilt is the most common strategy for keeping a rebellious person in tow. The
examples above are only a small sample of the multitude of statements and techniques for helping a son/
daughter to choose guilt (present-moment immobility
over a past event) as the price of genealogy.

Lover- and Spouse-Related Guilt

The "If you loved me" guilt is one way to manipulate
a lover. This tactic is particularly useful when one
wants to punish a partner for some particular behavior.
As if love were contingent upon the right kind of be-

havior. Whenever one person doesn't measure up, guilt can be used to get him back into the fold. He must feel guilty for not having loved the other.

Grudges, long silences and hurtful looks are useful methods of engendering guilt. "I'm not talking to you, that'll fix you" or "Don't come near me, how do you expect me to be loving after what you've done?" This is a commonly employed tactic in the case of straying behavior on the part of one partner.

Often, years after an incident, an action is recalled to help the other person to choose present-moment guilt. "But don't forget what you did in 1951" or "How could I ever trust you again, when you let me down before?" In this way one partner can manipulate the other's present with references to the past. If one partner has finally forgotten it, the other can periodically bring it up to keep the guilt feelings about the past behavior current.

Guilt is useful in making a love partner conform to the other's demands and standards of behavior. "If you were responsible, you would have called me" or "That's the third time I had to empty the garbage, I guess you just refuse to do your share." The goal? Getting one partner to do what the other wants him to. The method? Guilt.

Children-Inspired Guilt

The parental guilt game can be reversed. Guilt can be a two-way street and children are just as apt to use it in manipulating their parents as the reverse.

If a child realizes that his parent cannot cope with his being unhappy and will feel guilty for being a bad parent, the child will often try to use that guilt to manipulate the parent. A tantrum in the supermarket may produce the desired candy. "Sally's father lets her do it." Therefore Sally's father is a good father and you're not. "You don't love me. If you did you wouldn't treat me this way." And the ultimate, "I must be adopted. My real parents wouldn't treat me like this." All these statements carry the same message. You as a parent ought to feel guilty for treating me, your child, in this way.

Of course, children learn this guilt-producing behavior by watching the adults in their world use it to get things that they want. Guilt is not a natural behavior. It is a learned emotional response that can only be used if the victim teaches the exploiter that he is vulnerable. Children know when you are susceptible. If they constantly remind you of things that you've done, or haven't done, for the purpose of getting what they want, then they have learned the guilt trick. If your children use these tactics, they picked them up somewhere. Very likely, from you.

School-Inspired Guilt

Teachers are superlative guilt originators, and children, since they are most suggestible, are excellent subjects for manipulation. These are some of the guilt messages that produce present-moment unhappiness for young people:

"Your mother is really going to be disappointed in you."

"You should be ashamed of yourself for getting a C—a smart boy like you."

"How could you hurt your parents like that, after all they've done for you? Don't you know how badly they want you to go to Harvard?"

"You failed the test because you didn't study, now you'll have to live with yourself."

Guilt is often used in schools to make children learn certain things or behave in certain ways. And remember that even as an adult you are a product of those schools.

Church-Related Guilt

Religion is often used to produce guilt and therefore manipulate behavior. Here God is generally the one you have let down. In some cases the message is that you will be kept out of heaven for having behaved badly.

"If you loved God, you wouldn't behave that way."

"You won't get into heaven unless you repent for your sins."

"You should feel bad because you haven't gone to church every week, and if you feel bad enough, perhaps you'll be forgiven."

"You've disobeyed one of God's rules and you should feel ashamed of yourself."

Other Institutional Guilt Producers

Most prisons operate on the guilt theory. That is, if a person sits long enough thinking how bad he's been, he will be better for the guilt. Jail sentences for nonviolent crimes such as tax evasion, traffic citations, civil infractions and the like are examples of this mind-set. The fact that a strikingly large percentage of inmates return to law-breaking behavior has done nothing to challenge this belief.

Sit in a jail and feel bad for what you've done. This policy is so expensive and useless that it defies logical explanation. The illogical explanation, of course, is that *guilt* is such an integral part of our culture, that it is the backbone of our criminal justice system. Rather than have civil law breakers help society or repay their debts, they are reformed through guilt-producing incarceration that has no benefit to anyone, least of all the offender.

No amount of guilt, however large, will change past

behavior. Moreover, jails are not places where new legal choices are learned. Instead, they encourage a repetition of illegal behavior by embittering the prisoner. (The policy of imprisoning dangerous criminals to protect others is a different issue, and not under discussion here.)

In our society tipping is a practice that has come to reflect not superior service but the guilt of the person served. Effective waiters and waitresses, cab drivers, bellboys, and other serving employees have learned that most people cannot handle guilt for not behaving in the correct way and will tip the standard percentage regardless of the quality of service received. Thus blatant hand extending, nasty comments and looks that are designed to wither are all used to produce guilt and, fast on its heels, the big tip.

Littering, smoking and other unacceptable behavior may be things that you can be made to feel guilty about. Perhaps you've dropped a cigarette or a paper cup. A stern look by a stranger can send you into paroxysms of guilt for having behaved in such a crass fashion. Instead of feeling guilty about something you have already done, why not simply resolve not to behave in an antisocial manner again.

Dieting is an area that is loaded with guilt. The dieter eats one cookie and feels bad for a day for having been weak for a moment. If you are striving to lose weight and give in to counterproductive behavior, you can learn from it and work at being more effective in your present moment. But to feel guilty and full of self-reproach is a waste of time, for, if you feel that way for very long, you are likely to repeat the excess eating, as your own neurotic way out of your dilemma.

Sexual Expression Guilt

Perhaps the area where guilt flourishes best in our society is in the realm of sex. We have already seen how parents engender guilt in children for sexual acts or thoughts. Adults feel no less guilty about matters of sex. People sneak into porno films so that others won't know how bad they've been. Some people can't admit to enjoying oral sex and often feel guilty for even thinking about it.

Sexual fantasies are also effective guilt producers. Many feel bad about having such thoughts and deny their existence even in private, or in therapy. In fact, if I had to locate a guilt center in the body, I would place it in the crotch.

This is only a brief listing of the cultural influences that conspire to help you choose guilt. Now let's take a look at the psychological payoffs for feeling guilt. Keep in mind that whatever the dividend, it is bound to be self-defeating, and remember that the next time you opt for guilt over freedom.

The Psychological Payoffs for Choosing Guilt

Here are the most basic reasons for choosing to waste your present feeling guilty about things that you've done or failed to do in the past.

• By absorbing your present moments feeling guilty about something that has already taken place, you don't have to use that now moment in any kind of effective, self-enhancing way. Very simply, like so many self-defeating behaviors, guilt is an avoidance technique for working on yourself in the present. Thus you shift responsibility for what you are or are not now to what you were or were not in the past.

• By shifting responsibility backward you not only avoid the hard work of changing yourself now but the attendant risks that go with change as well. It is easier to immobilize yourself with guilt about the past than to take the hazardous path of growing in the present.

• There is a tendency to believe that if you feel guilty enough, you will eventually be exonerated for having been naughty. This being forgiven payoff is the basis of the prison mentality described above, in which the inmate pays for sins by feeling terrible for a long period of time. The greater the transgression, the longer the period of remorse necessary for pardon.

• Guilt can be a means of returning to the safety of childhood, a secure period when others made decisions for you and took care of you. Rather than taking yourself in hand in the present, you rely on the values of others from your past. And once again the payoff is in being protected from having to take charge of your own life.

• Guilt is a useful method for transferring responsibility for your behavior from yourself to others. It is easy to get infuriated at how you are being manipulated and to shift the focus for your guilt off yourself, and onto those infernal others, who are so powerful that they can make you feel anything they want, including guilt.

• Often you can win the approval of others even when those others don't approve of your behavior by feeling guilt for that behavior. You may have done something out of line, but by feeling guilty you are showing that you know the proper way to behave, and are making an attempt to fit in.

• Guilt is a superb way to win pity from others. No matter that the desire for the pity is a clear indication of low self-esteem. In this case you'd rather have others feel sorry for you, than like and respect yourself.

There you have the most notorious of the dividends for hanging onto guilt. Guilt, like all self-nullifying emotions, is a choice, something that you exercise control over. If you don't like it, and would prefer to make it go away so that you are entirely "guilt-free" here are some beginning strategies for wiping your guilt slate clean.

Some Strategies for Eliminating Guilt

• Begin to view the past as something that can never be changed, despite how you feel about it. It's over! And any guilt that you choose will not make the past different. Emblazon this sentence on your consciousness. "My feeling guilty will not change the past, nor will it make me a better person." This sort of thinking will help you to differentiate guilt from learning as a result of your past.

• Ask yourself what you are avoiding in the present with guilt about the past. By going to work on that particular thing, you will eliminate the need for guilt.

A client of mine who had been carrying on an extramarital affair for some time provides a good example of this kind of guilt elimination. The man professed to feel guilty about the affair, but continued to sneak away from his wife each week to see the other woman. I pointed out to him that the guilt he spoke so much about was a totally futile emotion. It did not improve his marriage and even prevented him from enjoying his affair. He had two choices. He could recognize that he was devoting his present to feeling guilty because it was easier than examining his marriage closely and going to work on it—and himself.

Or he could learn to accept his behavior. He could admit that he condoned extramarital sexual exploration and realize that his value system encompassed behavior which many people condemn. In either case, he would be choosing to eliminate the guilt, and to either change or accept himself.

• Begin to accept certain things about yourself that you've chosen but which others may dislike. Thus, if your parents, boss, neighbors, or even spouse, take a stand against some of your behavior, you can see that as natural. Remember what was said earlier about approval seeking. It is necessary that you approve of yourself; the approval of others is pleasant but beside the point. Once you no longer need approval, the guih for behavior which does not bring approval will disappear.

• Keep a *Guilt Journal* and write down any guilty moments, noting precisely when, why, and with whom it occurs, and what you are avoiding in the present with this agonizing over the past. The journal should provide some helpful insights into your particular guilt zone.

• Reconsider your value system. Which values do you believe in and which do you only pretend to accept? List all of these phony values and resolve to live up to a code of ethics that is self-determined, not one that has been imposed by others.

• Make a list of all the bad things you've ever done. Give yourself guilt points for each of them on a scale of one to ten. Add up your score and see if it makes any difference in the present whether it's one hundred or one million. The present moment is still the same and all of your guilt is merely wasteful activity.

• Assess the real consequences of your behavior. Rather than looking for a mystical feeling to determine yes's and no's in your life, determine whether the results of your actions are pleasing and productive for you.

• Teach those in your life who attempt to manipulate you with guilt that you are perfectly capable of handling their disappointment in you. Thus, if Mama gets into her guilt act with "You didn't do this" or "I'll get the chairs, you just sit there," learn new responses like "Okay, Mom, if you want to risk your back on a few chairs because you can't wait a few minutes, I guess there is little I can do to dissuade you." It will take some time, but their behavior will begin to change once they see they cannot force you to choose guilt. Once you de-fuse the guilt, the emotional control over you and the possibility of manipulation are eliminated forever.

• Do something which you know is bound to result in feelings of guilt. As you check into a hotel, and a bellboy is assigned to show you to a room that you are perfectly capable of finding alone with your one small piece of luggage, announce that you'll do it alone. If you're rejected, tell your unwanted companion that he is wasting his time and energy since you will not be leaving a tip for a service that you don't want. Or take a week to be alone if you've always wanted to do so, despite the guilt-engendering protestations from other members of your family. These kinds of behavior will help you to tackle that omnipresent guilt that so many sectors of the environment are adept at helping you to choose.

• The following dialogue represents a role-working exercise in a counseling group led by myself, in which a young girl (23) was confronting her mother (being played by another group member) about wanting to leave the nest. The mother was using every conceivable guilt-producing response to keep her from leaving home. This dialogue was the end product of an hour of teaching the daughter how to outmaneuver her mother's guilt-producing statements.

DAUGHTER: Mother—I'm leaving home.

MOTHER: If you do, I'll have a heart attack, you know how my heart is, and how I need you to help me with my medicine and all.

DAUGHTER: You're concerned about your health and you think you can't make it without me.

MOTHER: Of course I can't. Look, I've been good to you all these years, and now you're just walking out, leaving me here to die. If that's all you think of your mother, go ahead.

DAUGHTER: You think that because you've helped me as a child that I should repay you by staying here and not become independent and be on my own.

MOTHER: (Clutching at her chest) I'm having a tachycardia attack right now. I think

> I'm going to die. You're killing me,
> that's what you're doing.
>
> DAUGHTER: Is there anything you'd like to say to
> me before you leave?

In this dialogue, the daughter refused to yield to the obvious guilt producers offered by her mother. The daughter had been a literal slave, and any effort to be on her own had always been met with guilt-engendering talk. Mama was willing to use anything to keep her daughter dependent and in her control, and the daughter either had to learn new responses or be a slave to her mother and her own guilt for the rest of her life. Take careful notice of the daughter's responses. They all begin with references to her mother as responsible for her own feelings. By saying "You feel," rather than "I feel," the potential for guilt is tactfully minimized.

Such is guilt in our culture—a convenient tool for manipulating others and a futile waste of time. Worry, the other side of the coin, is diagnostically identical to guilt, but focuses exclusively on the future and all of the terrible things that *might* happen.

A Closer Look at Worry

There is nothing to worry about! Absolutely nothing. You can spend the rest of your life, beginning right now, worrying about the future, and no amount of your worry will change a thing. Remember that worry is defined as being immobilized in the present as a result of things that are going or not going to happen in the future. You must be careful not to confuse worrying with planning for the future. If you are planning, and the present-moment activity will contribute to a more effective future, then this is not worry. It is worry only when you are in any way immobilized now about a future happening.

Just as our society fosters guilt, so it encourages worry. Once again it all begins with equating worrying with caring. If you care about someone, the message goes, then you are bound to worry about the person. Thus, you'll hear sentences like, "Of course I'm worried, it's only natural when you care about someone" or "I can't help worrying, it's because I love you." Thus, you prove your love by doing an appropriate amount of worrying at the correct time.

Worry is endemic to our culture. Almost everyone spends an inordinate amount of present moments worrying about the future. And all of it is for naught. Not one moment of worry will make things any better. In fact, worry will very likely help you to be less effective in dealing with the present. Moreover, worry has nothing to do with love which predicates a relationship in which each person has the right to be what he chooses without any necessary conditions imposed by the other.

Think of yourself as being alive in 1860, at the beginning of the Civil War. The country is mobilizing for war, and there are approximately thirty-two million people in the United States. Each of those thirty-two million folks has hundreds of things to worry about and they spend many present moments agonizing about the future. They worry about war, the price of food, the draft, the economy, all the things that you worry about today. In 1975, some 115 years later, all of those worriers are dead and all their combined worrying did not change a moment of what is now history. The same is true of your own worry times. When the earth is populated by an entirely new crew, will any of your worry moments have made a difference? No. And, do any of your worry times make a difference today, in terms of changing the things you worry about? No, again. Then this is one zone that you must tidy up, since you are just wasting those precious present moments on behavior that has absolutely no positive payoff for you.

Much of your worry concerns things over which you have no control. You can worry all you want about war, or the economy, or possible illness, but worry won't bring peace or prosperity or health. As an individual you have little control over any of those things. Moreover the catastrophe you're worrying about frequently turns out to be less horrible in reality than it was in your imagination.

I worked with Harold, who was forty-seven years old, for several months. He was worried about being laid off and not being able to support his family. He was a compulsive worrier. He began losing weight, was unable to sleep and was getting sick frequently. In counseling, we talked about the futility of worry and how he could choose to be content. But Harold was a true worrier, and he felt that it was his responsibility to worry about possible impending disaster every day. Finally, after months of worry, he did receive his pink slip and was unemployed for the first time in his life. Within three days, he had secured another position, one which paid more, and gave him a great deal more satisfaction. He had used his compulsiveness to find the new job. His search was rapid and relentless. And all of his worry had been useless. His family had not starved, and Harold had not collapsed. Like most worry-producing gloom pictures in one's head, the eventuality resulted in benefits, rather than horror. Harold learned firsthand the futility of worry, and he has actually begun to adopt a nonworry stance in his life.

In a clever essay on worry in *The New Yorker*, entitled "Look for the Rusty Lining," Ralph Schoenstein satirizes worry.

What a list! Something old and something new, something cosmic yet something trivial too, for the creative worrier must forever blend the pedestrian with the immemorial. If the sun burns out, will the Mets be able to play their entire schedule at night? If cryogenically frozen human beings are ever revived, will they have to re-register to vote? And if the little toe disappears, will field goals play a smaller part in the National Football League?*

You may be in the professional worrier classification, creating unnecessary stress and anxiety in your life as a result of the choices you are making to worry about every conceivable kind of activity. Or you may be a minor league worrier concerned only about your own personal problems. The following list represents the most common responses to the question, "What do you worry about?"

Typical Worry Behaviors in Our Culture

I gathered the following data from some two hundred adults at a lecture one evening. I call this your worry sheet, and you can give yourself "worry points" similar to the "guilt points" discussed above. They are not listed in any particular sequence of frequency or importance. The parenthetical statements represent the kinds of sentences that justify the worry.

YOUR WORRY SHEET

I worry about . . .

1. *My children* ("Everyone worries about their children, I wouldn't be a very good parent if I didn't, now would I?")
2. *My health* ("If you don't worry about your health, you could die at any time!")
3. *Dying* ("No one wants to die. Everyone worries about death.")
4. *My job* ("If you don't worry about it, you might lose it.")
5. *The economy* ("Someone ought to worry about it, the President doesn't seem to care.")

* Ralph Schoenstein, "Look for the Rusty Lining," *The New Yorker* (Feb. 3, 1975).

6. *Having a heart attack* ("Everyone does, don't they?" "Your heart could go at any minute.")

7. *Security* ("If you don't worry about security, you'll find yourself in the poorhouse, or on welfare.")

8. *My wife's/husband's happiness* ("God knows I spend a lot of time worrying about him/her being happy, and they still don't appreciate it.")

9. *Am I doing the right thing?* ("I always worry about doing things right, that way I know I'm okay.")

10. *Having a healthy child if you're pregnant* ("Every mother-to-be worries about that.")

11. *Prices* ("Somebody ought to worry about them before they skyrocket out of sight.")

12. *Accidents* ("I always worry that my spouse or the children will have an accident. It's only natural, isn't it?")

13. *What others will think* ("I worry about my friends not liking me.")

14. *My weight* ("No one wants to be fat, so naturally I worry about not gaining back any of the weight I lost.")

15. *Money* ("We never seem to have enough, and I worry that someday we'll be broke and have to go on welfare.")

16. *My car breaking down* ("It's an old clunker and I drive it on the expressway, so of course I worry about it and what might happen if it did.")

17. *My bills* ("Everyone worries about paying their bills. You wouldn't be human if you didn't worry about bills.")

18. *My parents dying* ("I don't know what I'd do if they died, it worries me sick. I worry about being alone, I don't think I could handle it.")

19. *Getting into heaven or what if there is no God*

("I can't stand the idea of there being nothing.")

20. *The weather* ("I plan things like a picnic and maybe it'll rain. I worry about having snow for skiing.")

21. *Getting old* ("No one wants to get old, and you can't kid me, everyone worries about that one." "I don't know what I'll do when I retire and I really worry about that.")

22. *Flying* ("You hear about all those plane crashes.")

23. *My daughter's virginity* ("Every father who loves his daughter worries that she'll be hurt, or get into trouble.")

24. *Talking in front of groups* ("I get petrified in front of a crowd and I worry like crazy before I do it.")

25. *When my spouse doesn't call* ("It seems normal to me to worry when you don't know where someone you love is, or if they're in trouble.")

26. *Going into the city* ("Who knows what'll happen in the jungle. I worry every time I go in." "I always worry about whether I'll get a parking space.")

And perhaps the most neurotic of all . . .

27. *Having nothing to worry about* ("I can't just sit still when everything seems all right, I worry about not knowing what will happen next.")

This is the collective worry sheet of people in our culture. You can give worry points to each of those that seem most applicable to you, total it up, and no matter what your score, it still adds up to zero. The following paragraph illustrates the extent of worry in our world. It's taken from a story in *Newsday* (May 3, 1975) on hospital malpractice insurance.

West Islip—Two officials of the Nassau-Suffolk Hospital Council warned yesterday that those *worrying* about the problems that the malpractice insurance crisis could create—if doctors cease treating patients entirely or treat only emergency cases—have not *worried* quite enough.

Indeed, a call to spend more time worrying about a problem. How could a story like this even appear? Because the cultural pressure is to worry, rather than to do. If all of those concerned were to worry a lot more, perhaps the problem would go away.

In order to eliminate worry it is necessary to understand the why behind it. If worry is a large part of your life, you can bet that it has many historical antecedents. But what are the payoffs? They are similar to the neurotic dividends that you receive for guilt, since both worry and guilt are self-nullifying behaviors, that vary only in a temporal sense. Guilt focuses on the past; worry on the future.

The Psychological Payoffs for Choosing Worry

• Worry is a present-moment activity. Thus, by using your current life being immobilized over a future time in your life, you are able to escape the now and whatever it is in the now that threatens you. For example, I spent the summer of 1974 in Karamursel, Turkey, teaching and writing a book on counseling. My seven-year-old daughter was back in the United States with her mother. While I love writing, I also find it an intensely lonely, difficult chore which requires a great deal of self-discipline. I would sit down at my typewriter with paper in place and the margins set, and all of a sudden my thoughts would be back on little Tracy Lynn. What if she rides her bicycle into the street and doesn't look? I hope she's being watched at the swimming pool, because she has a tendency to be careless. Before I knew it, an hour had elapsed, and I had spent it worrying. This was all in vain of course. But, was it? As long as I could use up my present moments worrying I didn't have to struggle with the difficulty of writing. A terrific payoff indeed.

• You can avoid having to take risks by using your worry as the reason for immobility. How could you possibly act if you are preoccupied with your present-moment worry? "I can't do a thing, I'm just too worried about——." This is a common lament, and one with a payoff that keeps you standing still and avoiding the risk of action.

• You can label yourself as a *caring person* by worrying. Worry proves that you are a good parent, good spouse, or good whatever. A handsome dividend, although lacking in logical healthy thinking.

• Worry is a handy justification for certain self-defeating behavior. If you're overweight, you undoubtedly eat more when you worry, hence you have a sensational reason for hanging on to the worry behavior. Similarly, you find yourself smoking more in worrisome situations, and can use the worry to avoid giving up smoking. This same neurotic reward system applies to areas including marriage, money, health and the like. The worry helps you to avoid changing. It is easier to worry about chest pains than to take the risk of finding out the truth, and then have to deal forthrightly with yourself.

• Your worry keeps you from living. A worrier sits around and thinks about things, while a doer must be up and about. Worry is a clever device to keep you inactive, and clearly it is easier, if less rewarding, to worry, than to be an active, involved person.

• Worry can bring ulcers, hypertension, cramps, tension headaches, backaches and the like. While these may not seem to be payoffs, they do result in considerable attention from others and justify much self-pity as well, and some people would rather be pitied than fulfilled.

❉　　❉　　❉

Now that you understand the psychological support system for your worry, you can begin to devise some strategic efforts for getting rid of the troublesome worry bugs that breed in this erroneous zone.

Some Strategies for Eliminating Worry

• Begin to view your present moments as times to live, rather than to obsess about the future. When you catch yourself worrying, ask yourself, "What am I avoiding now by using up this moment with worry?" Then begin to attack whatever it is you're avoiding. The best antidote to worry is action. A client of mine, formerly prone to worry, told me of a recent triumph over it. At a vacation resort he wandered into the sauna one afternoon. There he met a man who couldn't take a holiday from his worries. The other man elaborated all of the things my client should be worrying about. He mentioned the stock market, but said not to worry about short-range fluctuations. In six months there would be a virtual collapse, and that was the thing to really worry about. My client made sure of all the things he should worry about, and then left. He played a one-hour game of tennis, enjoyed a touch football game with some young children, participated with his wife in a Ping-Pong match which they thoroughly enjoyed, and finally, some three hours later, returned for a shower/sauna. His new friend was still there worrying, and began once again to chronicle more things to worry about. Meantime, my client had spent his present moments excitedly alive, while the other man had consumed his in worry. And neither man's behavior had any effect on the stock market.

• Recognize the preposterousness of worry. Ask yourself over and over, "Is there anything that will ever change as a result of my worrying about it?"

• Give yourself shorter and shorter periods of "worry-time." Designate ten minutes in the morning and afternoon as your worry segments. Use these periods to fret about every potential disaster you can get into the time slot. Then, using your ability to control your own thoughts, postpone any further worry until your next designated "worry-time." You'll soon see the folly of using any time in this wasteful fashion, and will eventually eliminate your worry zone completely.

• Make a worry list of everything you worried about yesterday, last week and even last year. See if any of your worry did anything productive for you. Assess also how many of the things you worried about ever materialized at all. You'll soon see that the worry is really a doubly wasteful activity. It does nothing to alter the future. And the projected catastrophe often turns out to be minor, or even a blessing when it arrives.

• *Just Worry!* See if it is something that you can demonstrate when you are tempted to worry. That is, stop and turn to someone and say, "Watch me—I'm about to worry." They'll be confounded since you probably won't even know how to demonstrate the thing you do so well, so often.

• Ask yourself this worry-eradicating question, "What's the worst thing that could happen to me (or them) and what is the likelihood of it occurring?" You'll discover the absurdity of worry in this way.

• Deliberately choose to act in some manner that is in direct conflict with your usual areas of worry. If you compulsively save for the future, always worried about having enough money for another day, begin to use your money today. Be like the rich uncle who put in his will, "Being of sound mind, I spent all my money while I was alive."

• Begin to face the fears you possess with productive thought and behavior. A friend of mine recently spent a week on an island off the coast of Connecticut. The woman enjoys taking long walks, and soon discovered that the island was populated by many dogs who were allowed to run wild. She decided to fight her fear and worry that they might somehow bite her or even tear her limb from limb—the ultimate calamity. She carried a rock in her hand (insurance) and decided to show no sign of fear as the dogs approached. She even refused to slow down when the dogs growled and came running toward her. As the dogs charged forward and encountered someone who refused to back down, they gave up and ran away. While I am not advocating dangerous behavior, I do believe that an effective challenge to a fear or worry is the most productive way to eradicate it from your life.

These are some techniques for eliminating worry in your life. But the most effective weapon you have for wiping out worry is your own determination to banish this neurotic behavior from your life.

Final Thoughts on Worry and Guilt

The present moment is the key to understanding your guilt and worry activities. Learn to live now and not waste your current moments in immobilizing thoughts about the past or future. There is no other moment to live but now, and all of your futile guilt and worry are done in the elusive now.

Lewis Carroll in *Alice Through the Looking Glass* talked about living in the present.

"The rule is, jam tomorrow, and jam yesterday . . . but never jam today."
"It must come sometimes to 'jam-today,' " Alice objected.

How about you? Any jam today? Since it must come sometime, how about now?

VI
Exploring the
Unknown

Only the insecure strive for security.

You may be a safety expert—an individual who shuns the unknown in favor of always knowing where he is going, and what he can expect when he gets there. Early training in our society tends to encourage caution at the expense of curiosity, safety at the expense of adventure. Avoid the questionable, stay in areas that you know, never wander into the unknown. These early messages can become a psychological barrier that prevents your own personal fulfillment and present-moment happiness in countless ways.

Albert Einstein, a man who devoted his life to exploring the unknown, said in an article entitled "What I Believe" in *Forum* (October 1930),

> The most beautiful thing we can experience is the mysterious. It is the true source of all art and science.

He might also have said it is the source of all growth and excitement as well.

But too many people equate the unknown with danger. The purpose of life, they think, is to deal with certainty, and to always know where they are headed. Only the foolhardy risk exploring the fuzzy areas of life, and when they do, they end up being surprised, hurt, and worst of all, unprepared. As a young scout you were told to *Be Prepared*. But how can you prepare for the unknown? Obviously, you cannot! Therefore avoid it and you'll never end up with egg on your face. Be safe, don't take risks, follow the road maps—even if it is dull.

Perhaps you're getting tired of all that certainty, knowing what every day will be like before it has been lived. You can't grow if you already know the answers before the questions have even been asked. Probably the times you most remember are those in which you were spontaneously alive, doing whatever you wanted, and delightfully anticipating the mysterious.

We hear the cultural messages of certainty throughout life. They began with family and are reinforced by educators. The child learns to avoid experimentation and is encouraged to avoid the unknown. Don't get lost. Have the right answers. Stay with your own kind. If you still cling to these fearful encouragements to security, now is the time to break free. Get rid of the idea that you can't try out new and doubtful behavior. You can if you choose to. It begins with an understanding of your conditioned reflex to avoid new experiences.

Openness to New Experiences

If you believe in yourself fully, no activity is beyond your potential. The entire gamut of human experience is yours to enjoy, once you decide to venture into territory where you don't have guarantees. Think of the people who are regarded as geniuses and were spectacularly effective in their lifetimes. They weren't people who could do only one thing well. They weren't individuals who avoided the unknown. Benjamin Franklin, Ludwig van Beethoven, Leonardo da Vinci, Jesus Christ, Albert Einstein, Galileo, Bertrand Russell, George Bernard Shaw, Winston Churchill, these and many like them were pioneers, adventurers into new, unreliable areas. They were people, just like you, set apart only in that they were willing to traverse areas where others dared not tread. Albert Schweitzer, another Renaissance Man, once said, "Nothing human is alien to me." You can look at yourself with new eyes, and open yourself up to experiences that you've never even considered as a part of your own human potential, or you can do the same things, the same way, until you reach your coffin. It is a fact that great men remind you of no other, and their greatness is generally discernible in the quality of exploration and the boldness with which they explored the unknown.

Opening yourself up to new experiences means surrendering the notion that it is better to tolerate something familiar than to work at changing it because change is fraught with uncertainty. Perhaps you've adopted a stance that the self (you) is fragile, and easily shattered if you enter areas where you've never been before. This is a myth. You are a tower of strength. You are not going to collapse or fall apart if you encounter something new. In fact, you stand a much better chance of avoiding psychological collapse if you eliminate some of the routine and sameness in your life. Boredom is debilitating and psychologically unhealthy. Once you lose interest in life you are potentially shatterable. You won't choose that mythological nervous breakdown if you add a little spicy uncertainty to your life.

You may also have adopted the "if it's unusual I must stay away from it" mentality, which inhibits your openness to new experiences. Thus, if you see deaf people using sign language, you watch with curiosity but never attempt to converse with them. Similarly, when you encounter people who speak a foreign language, rather than work it out and attempt somehow to communicate, you very likely just wander off, and avoid the vast unknown of communicating in other than your own spoken language. There are uncountable activities and people who are considered taboo merely because they are unknown. Thus homosexuals, transvestites, the handicapped, the retarded, nudists and the like, are in the category of the obscure. You are not quite certain how to behave, and therefore you avoid the entire business.

You may also believe that you must have a reason for doing something; otherwise what's the point of doing it? Balderdash! You can do anything you want just because you want to, and for no other reason. You don't need a reason for anything that you do. Looking for a reason for everything is the kind of thinking that keeps you from new and exciting experiences. As a child you could play with a grasshopper for an hour, for no reason but that you liked it. Or you could climb a hill, or take an exploratory trip in the woods. Why? Because you wanted to. But as an adult, you have to come up with a good reason for things. This passion for reasons keeps you from opening up and growing. What freedom to know that you don't have to justify anything to anyone, including yourself, ever again.

Emerson, in his Journal of April 11, 1834, observed

> Four snakes gliding up and down a hollow for no purpose that I could see. Not to eat. Not for love . . . But only gliding.

You can do whatever you want because you want to and for no other reason. This kind of thinking will open up new vistas of experience and help to eliminate the fear of the unknown that you may have adopted as a life-style.

Rigidity vs. Spontaneity

Take a hard look at your spontaneity. Can you open up to something new or do you rigidly hang on to your accustomed behavior? Spontaneity means being able to try anything, at the spur of the second, just because it is something you'd enjoy. You may even discover that it's something you don't enjoy doing but you did enjoy attempting it. It is likely that you will be condemned as irresponsible or incautious, but what does the judgment of others matter when you're having such a marvelous time discovering the unknown. There are many people in high places who find it difficult to be spontaneous. They live out their lives in a rigid fashion, oblivious to the absurdities they blindly follow. Democrats and Republicans support the statements of top party leaders and vote the party line. Cabinet officials who speak spontaneously and honestly are very often ex-cabinet officials. Independent thinking is discouraged, and there are official guidelines for how one should think and speak. Yes-men are not spontaneous men. They desperately fear the unknown. They fit in. They do what they are told. They never challenge but rigidly adhere to what is expected of them. Where are you on this dimension? Can you be your own person in this area? Can you spontaneously take the avenues that don't always lead to a sure thing?

The rigid never grow. They tend to do things the same way they've always done them. A colleague of mine who teaches graduate courses for teachers frequently asks the old-timers, who have spent thirty years or more in the classroom, "Have you really been teaching for thirty years or have you been teaching one year, thirty times?" And you, dear reader, have you really lived 10,000 or more days or have you lived one day, 10,000 or more times? A good question to ask yourself as you work toward more spontaneity in your life.

Prejudice and Rigidity

Rigidity is the basis of all prejudice, which means to *pre*-judge. Prejudice is based less on hate or even dislike for certain people, ideas, or activities than on the fact that it's easier and safer to stay with the known. That is, people who are like you. Your prejudices seem to work for you. They keep you away from people, things and ideas that are unknown and potentially troublesome. Actually they work against you by preventing you from exploring the unknown. Being spontaneous means eliminating your pre-judgments and allowing yourself to meet and deal with new people and ideas. The pre-judgments themselves are a safety valve for avoiding murky or puzzling provinces and preventing growth. If you don't trust anyone you can't get a "handle on," it really means you don't trust yourself on unfamiliar grounds.

The "Always Having a Plan" Trap

There is no such thing as planned spontaneity. It is a contradiction in terms. We all know people who go through their lives with a road map and a list, unable to vary their life a single iota from the original plan. A plan is not necessarily unhealthy, but falling in love with the plan is the real neurosis. You may have a life plan for what you'll do at age 25, 30, 40, 50, 70, etc., and then you simply consult your agenda to see where you ought to be, rather than making a new decision each day and having a strong enough belief in yourself to be able to alter the plan. Don't let the plan become bigger than you.

Henry was a client of mine who was in his middle twenties. He suffered desperately from the having-a-plan-neurosis, and as a consequence he missed out on many exciting life opportunities. When he was twenty-two he was offered a position in another state. He was petrified about the move. Would he be able to make it in Georgia? Where would he live? How about his parents and friends? The fear of the unknown literally immobilized Henry, and he turned down what might have been a chance at advancement, exciting new work and a brand-new environment, in favor of staying where he was. It was this experience that brought Henry to counseling. He felt that his own rigid adherence to a plan was keeping him from growing, and yet he was afraid to break out and try something new. After one exploratory session, it was revealed that Henry was a veritable plan freak. He always ate the same breakfast, planned his clothing days in advance, had his dresser drawers arranged perfectly by color and size. Moreover, he imposed his plan on his family as well. He expected his children to have things in their place and his wife to conform to a rigid set of rules that he had laid down. In short, Henry was a very unhappy, albeit organized person. He lacked creativity, innovation and personal warmth. He was in fact, a plan unto himself, with his goal in life to get everything into its proper place. With counseling, Henry began to try some spontaneous living. He saw his plans as manipulators of others, and as convenient escapes from wandering into the risky unknown. He soon eased up on his family and allowed them to be different from what he expected them to be. After several months, Henry actually applied for a job in a firm that would require him to move frequently. The very thing that he originally feared became desirable. While Henry is by no means a totally spontaneous person, he has effectively challenged some of the neurotic thinking that supported his previously planned-out existence. He is working on it every day, and learning to enjoy living, rather than living out his life in a ritualized fashion.

Security: Internal and External Varieties

A long time ago you learned how to write a high school theme or essay. You were taught that you need a good introduction, a well-organized body and a conclusion. Unfortunately, you may have applied the same logic to your life, and come to see the whole business of living as a theme. The introduction was your childhood wherein you were preparing to be a person. The body is your adult life, which is organized and planned out in preparation for your conclusion, which is the retirement and happy ending. All of this organized thinking keeps you from living your present moments. Living according to this plan implies a guarantee that everything will be okay forever. Security, the final plan, is for cadavers. Security means knowing what is going to happen. Security means no excitement, no risks, no challenge. Security means no growth and no growth means death. Besides, security is a myth. As long as you are a person on earth, and the system stays the same, you can never have security. And even if it weren't a myth, it would be a horrible way to live. Certainty eliminates excitement—and growth.

The word security as used here refers to external guarantees, possessions such as money, a house and a car, to bulwarks such as a job or a position in the community. But there is a different kind of security that is worth pursuing, and this is the internal security of trusting yourself to handle anything that may come down the pike. This is the only lasting security, the only real security. Things can break down, a depression can wipe out your money, your house can be repossessed, but you, you can be a rock of self-esteem. You can believe so much in you and your internal strength that things or others will be seen as mere pleasant but superfluous adjuncts to your life.

Try this little exercise. Suppose that right now, this second, as you are reading this book, someone swooped down on you, stripped you naked, and carted you off in a helicopter. No warning, no money, nothing but yourself. Supposing you were flown to the middle of Red China and dropped in a field. You would be up against new language, new habits, and new climate, and all you would have is yourself. Would you survive or collapse? Could you make friends, get food, shelter and the like, or would you simply lie there and moan about how unfortunate you were to have this catastrophe visited on you? If you need external security, you'd perish, for all of your goods would have been taken away. But if you have internal security and are not afraid of the unknown, then you would survive.

Security can then be redefined as the knowledge that you can handle anything, including having no external security. Don't be trapped by that kind of external security, since it robs you of your ability to live and grow and fulfill yourself. Take a look at those people without external security, people who don't have it all mapped out. Perhaps they are way ahead of the game. At least they can try new things and avoid the trap of always having to stay with the safe.

James Kavanaugh in *Will You Be My Friend?* writes tellingly about security in his little poem called *Some Day*.

> Someday I'll walk away
>   And be free
> And leave the sterile ones
>   Their secure sterility.
> I'll leave without a forwarding address
> And walk across some barren wilderness
>   To drop the world there.
>   Then wander free of care
> Like an unemployed Atlas.*

Achievement as Security

But the "walking away" to "be free," as Kavanaugh puts it, is difficult as long as you carry around the conviction that you must achieve. Fear of failure is a powerful fear in our society, one inculcated in childhood and often carried throughout life.

You may be surprised to hear this, but failure does not exist. Failure is simply someone else's opinion of how a certain act should have been completed. Once you believe that no act must be performed in any specific other-directed way, then failing becomes impossible.

There may, however, be occasions when you will

* Los Angeles: Nash Publishing Corp., 1971.

fail in some given task according to your own standards. The important thing here is not to equate the act with your own self-worth. Not to succeed in a particular endeavor is not to fail as a person. It is simply not being successful with that particular trial at that particular present moment.

Try to imagine using failure as a description of an animal's behavior. Consider a dog barking for fifteen minutes, and someone saying, "He really isn't very good at barking, I'd give him a 'C.' How. absurd! It is impossible for an animal to fail because there is no provision for evaluating natural behavior. Spiders construct webs, not successful or unsuccessful webs. Cats hunt mice; if they aren't successful in one attempt, they simply go after another. They don't lie there and whine, complaining about the one that got away, or have a nervous breakdown because they failed. Natural behavior simply is! So why not apply the same logic to your own behavior and rid yourself of the fear of failure.

The push to achieve comes from three of the most self-destructive words in our culture. You've heard them and used them thousands of times. Do your best! This is the cornerstone of the achievement neurosis. Do your best at everything you do. What's wrong with taking a mediocre bicycle ride, or going for an average walk in the park? Why not have some activities in your life which you just do, rather than do to the best of your ability? The do-your-best neurosis can keep you from trying new activities and enjoying old ones.

At one time I counseled an eighteen-year-old high school senior named Louann, who was imbued with the achievement standard. Louann was a straight "A" student, and had been since she first set foot in a school. She worked long tedious hours on her school work, and as a result she had no time for being a person. She was a veritable computer of book knowledge. Yet Louann was painfully shy around boys, never even having held hands let alone dated. She had developed a nervous twitch which came into play whenever we talked about this side of her personality. Louann had placed all of her emphasis on being an achieving student at the expense of her total development. In working with Louann, I asked her what was more important in her life. "What you know, or how you feel?" Even though she was a valedictorian, she was lacking inner peace and was actually very unhappy. She began to place some importance on her feelings, and because she was such an excellent learner, she applied the same rigorous standards to learning new social behaviors as she had to her school work. Louann's mother called me a year later and told me that she was concerned because her daughter had received her very first "C" in a college freshman English class. I recommended that she make a big production out of it, and take her out for dinner in celebration.

Perfectionism

Why should you have to do everything well? Who is keeping score for you? Winston Churchill's famous lines about perfectionism indicate just how immobilizing the constant search for success can be.

The maxim "nothing avails but perfection" may be spelled P A R A L Y S I S

You can paralyze yourself with perfectionistic do-your-best nonsense. Perhaps you can give yourself some significant areas in your life in which you truly want to do your best. But in the vast majority of activities, having to do your best, or even to do well, is an obstacle to doing. Don't let perfectionism keep you on the sidelines avoiding potentially pleasurable activities. Try changing "Do your best" to simply "Do."

Perfection means immobility. If you have perfect standards for yourself, then you'll never try anything and you won't do much because perfect is not a concept that applies to human beings. God can be perfect, but you, as a person, need not apply such ridiculous standards to you and your behavior.

If you have children, don't breed paralysis and resentment by insisting they do their best. Instead, talk with them about the things they seem to enjoy the most, and perhaps give some encouragement to try hard in those areas. But in other activities, doing is so much more important than succeeding. Teach them to play in the volleyball game rather than sit on the sidelines saying "I'm no good." Encourage them to ski, or to sing, or draw, or dance or whatever, because they want to, not to avoid something just because they may not be good at it. No one should be taught to be competitive, to try, or even to do well. Instead, try to teach the lessons of self-esteem and pride and pleasure in the activities deemed important by the individual.

A child is easily taught the ugly message of equating his own self-worth with his failures. Consequently he will begin to shun activities in which he does not excel. Even more dangerous, he may develop habits of low self-esteem, approval-seeking, guilt and all of the erroneous zone behaviors that go with self-rejection.

If you equate your worth with your failures and successes, you'll be doomed to feelings of worthlessness. Think of Thomas Edison. If he'd used failure in any given task as an indicator of his own self-esteem, after his first trial in which he failed he would have given up on himself, announced that he was a failure and ceased his endeavors to light the world. Failure can be instructive, it can be an incentive to work and exploration. It can even be thought of as success if it points the way to new discoveries. As Kenneth Boulding put it,

> I have revised some folk wisdom lately; one of my edited proverbs is *Nothing fails like success* because you do not learn anything from it. The only thing we ever learn from is failure. Success only confirms our superstitions.

Think of it. Without failure we can learn nothing, and yet we have learned to treasure success as the only acceptable standard. We tend to shun all experiences which might bring about failure. Apprehension of failure is a big part of fear of the unknown. Anything which doesn't smack of guaranteed success is to be avoided. And fearing failure means fearing both the unknown and the disapproval that accompanies not doing your best.

Some Typical "Fear of the Unknown" Behavior in Our Culture

We have already discussed some typical behavior engendered by fear of the unknown. Resisting new experiences, rigidity, prejudice, slavish adherence to plans, the need for external security, fear of failure and perfectionism are all subheadings in this large self-limiting zone. What follows is a listing of the most common specific examples in this category. You can use it as a checklist to assess your own behavior.

• Eating the same kinds of foods for a lifetime. Avoiding exotic, new taste treats in favor of the more traditional, and using descriptions such as, "I'm a meat and potatoes person" or "I always order chicken." While everyone has certain preferences and predilections, avoidance of unknown foods is merely rigidity. Some people have never eaten a taco, or been to a Greek or Indian restaurant, simply because they stay on the familiar ground of what they are used to. Leaving familiar grounds can open up a whole exciting gastronomic world.

• Wearing the same kinds of clothes forever. Never trying out a new style, or wearing something different. Labeling yourself as a "conservative dresser" or a "loud dresser" and never varying your sartorial style.

• Reading the same newspapers and magazines which support the same editorial position day after day and never admitting a contrary viewpoint. In one recent study, a reader, whose political position was well known, was asked to read an editorial which began with a position identical to his own. In the middle of the editorial, the viewpoint shifted, and a hidden camera revealed that the reader's eyes similarly shifted to another part of the page. The rigid reader in this experiment would not even consider a dissimilar point of view.

• Seeing the same movies (with different titles) for a lifetime. Refusing to view anything that might support a different philosophical or political belief, because the unknown is disconcerting and must be shut out.

• Living in the same neighborhood, city or state, simply because your parents and their parents happened to have chosen that location. Being afraid of a new place because the people, climate, politics, language, customs, or whatever, are different.

• Refusing to listen to ideas which you do not share. Instead of considering the other speaker's viewpoint— "Hmm, I've never thought of that"—you immediately insist he's crazy or uninformed. This is a method of avoiding the different or the unknown by refusing to communicate.

• Being afraid to try a new activity because you can't do it well. "I don't think I'd be very good, I'll just watch."

• Compulsive achievement in school or on the job. Grades are more important than anything else. The fitness report matters more than the pleasure of work well done. Using achievement rewards as substitutes for trying something new and unknown. Residing in the safe areas of inquiry because, "I know I can get an 'A,'" rather than risking a "C" by embarking on a new discipline. Taking the safe job where you know you'll be successful instead of entering a new race and taking a chance on failing.

• Avoiding anyone whom you label deviant, including "fags," "commies," "weirdos," "spics," "niggers," "wops," "wasps," "hippies," "kikes," "gooks," and any derogatory tags that serve as protection from fear of the unfamiliar. Rather than trying to learn about these people, you label them with a slanderous epithet and talk about them rather than to them.

• Staying with the same job even though you dislike it, not because you have to, but out of apprehension about entering that vast unknown of new work.

• Staying in a marriage that obviously is not working, out of a fear of the unknown, single life. You can't remember what it's like not to be married, so you don't know what you'd be getting yourself into. Better to stay with the unpleasant familiar than to wander off into new potentially lonely territory.

• Taking vacations in the same place, at the same hotel, during the same season each year. In this case you know what to expect, and you don't have to risk new places which might—or might not—provide pleasant experiences.

• Using performance rather than enjoyment as a criterion for everything that you do. That is, doing only those things you do well and avoiding those where you might fail or perform poorly.

• Measuring things in monetary terms. If it costs more, it is worth more, and therefore an indication of your personal success. The known is measured in dollar signs, while the unknown cannot be financially assessed.

• Striving for the important title, the fancy automobiles, the right labels on your clothes and other status symbols, even though you may not even like the possessions and the life-style that they represent.

• An inability to alter a plan when an interesting alternative arises. If you stray from the map in your head you'll lose your way and your place in life.

• Being preoccupied with time, and allowing clocks to run your life. Living by a schedule which keeps you from trying new and unknown quantities of life. Always wearing a watch (even to bed) and being controlled by it. Sleeping, eating and making love by the clock, regardless of hunger, exhaustion, or desire.

• Dismissing certain kinds of activities which you've never tried. These may include such "weird" things as meditation, yoga, astrology, backgammon, bocci, Mah-jongg, isometrics, or anything that you don't know about.

• Viewing sex without imagination. Always doing the same thing in the same position. Never trying something new and exotic, because it is different and therefore might be unacceptable.

• Hiding behind the same clique of friends and never branching out with different people who represent new and unknown worlds. Having regular meetings with the same crowd, and staying with the crowd for a lifetime.

• At a party which you attend with your spouse or date, staying with that person for the entire evening not because you want to but because you are safe.

• Hanging back because of a fear of what might happen if you ventured into a conversation with strange people on strange topics. Thinking to yourself that they must be smarter, more talented, more skillful, or more glib, and using this as a reason to avoid a new experience.

• Condemning yourself if you don't succeed in all your endeavors.

These are only a few examples of unhealthy behavior engendered by fear of the unknown. You can probably make your own list. But instead of making lists, why not begin to challenge why you want to live each day the same as the one before, with no possibilities for growth.

The Psychological Support System for Retaining These Behaviors

Here are some common payoffs that keep you from roaming around in that delicious unknown.

• By staying the same you never have to think on your feet. If you have a good plan, you simply consult your script, rather than your wits.

• Staving off the unknown has its own built-in reward system. The fear of the obscure is strong, and as long as you stay with the familiar, you are keeping that fear at bay, regardless of how costly it is to you in growth and fulfillment. It's safer to avoid uncharted areas. Think of Columbus. Everyone warned him he would fall over the edge. It is easier to be one of the many treading familiar ground rather than an explorer risking everything. The unknown is a challenge and challenges can be threats.

• You can say that you are postponing your gratification, which you've heard labeled "mature-behavior," and thus stay with the familiar and justify it with such a stance. Thus it is "mature" and "adult" to put it off, but really it is out of panic and misgiving that you stay as you are, and avoid unknown parts.

• You can feel important by having done it right. You've been a good boy/girl. As long as you see it in failure/success terms, you can equate your self-worth with your good performance and feel good. But the right thing in this sense is only someone else's editorial opinion.

Some Strategies for Coming to Grips with the Mysterious and the Unknown

• Make selective efforts to try new things even if you are tempted to stay with the familiar. For example, at a restaurant order a new dish. Why? Because it would be different and you might enjoy it.

• Invite a collection of people to your home who represent widely divergent points of view. Go with the unknown rather than your typical clique of acquaintances wherein you can predict everything that will take place.

• Give up having to have a reason for everything you do. When someone asks you why, remember that you don't have to come up with a reasonable answer that will satisfy them. You can do what you decide just because you want to.

• Begin to take some risks that will get you out of your routine. Perhaps an unplanned vacation with no reservations or maps, where you just trust yourself to handle whatever might come along. Interview for a new job, or talk with someone that you've been avoiding because you were afraid of not knowing what might happen. Take a new route to work, or have dinner at midnight. Why? Just because it's different and you want to do it.

• Entertain yourself with a fantasy in which you allow yourself to have anything you want. No holds barred. You have all of the money to do anything you want for a two-week period. You'll find that almost all of your mental meanderings are indeed attainable for you, that you don't want the moon or the unreachable, but simply things that you can achieve if you eliminate the fear of the unknown and go after them.

• Take a risk that might involve some personal up-heaval, but which would be intensely rewarding to you. For several years a colleague of mine had told his students and clients about the need for trying the un-known in their lives. But in many ways his advice was hypocritical since he stayed with the same university, consulting work and comfortable life-style. He had stated that anyone could handle new and different situations, but he continued to stay with the familiar. In 1974 he decided to live in Europe for six months be-cause it was something he had always wanted to do. He taught two courses for an overseas graduate pro-gram in educational psychology and learned firsthand (experientially rather than verbally) that he could han-dle the doubtful. After three weeks in Germany, be-cause of his inner security, he had as many opportunities to conduct workshops, work with clients and give lec-tures as he had had in New York where he was comfortable with the familiar surroundings. Even in a remote village in Turkey, where he lived for two months, he was busier than he had been in New York.

At last, out of experience, he knew that he could go anywhere, at any time, and be effective, not because of the external circumstances, but because he could handle the unknown, exactly as he handled the known, with his own inner strength and skills.

• Whenever you find yourself avoiding the unknown, ask yourself, "What's the worst thing that could happen to me?" You'll probably see that the fears of the unknown are out of proportion to the reality of the consequences.

• Try to do something silly like going barefoot in the park, or skinny-dipping. Try out some of the things that you've always avoided because you "Mustn't ever do such things." Open your own personal horizons to new experiences that you've previously avoided because they were silly or inane.

• Remind yourself that the fear of failure is very often the fear of someone else's disapproval or ridicule. If you let them have their own opinions, which have nothing to do with you, you can begin to evaluate your behavior in your own, rather than their terms. You'll come to see your abilities not as better or worse, but as simply different from others.

• Make an attempt to do some things that you've always avoided, with the sentence "I'm just not good at that." You can spend an afternoon painting a picture and have a hell of a time. If the end product is less than masterful, you haven't failed, you've had a half day of pleasure. On my living room wall is a painting that is aesthetically horrible. Everyone who visits comments or painfully avoids commenting on how bad it really is. In the lower left-hand corner are inscribed the words, "To you, Dr. Dyer, I give you not my best." It is from a former student who had avoided painting all of her life because she'd learned a long time ago that she was bad at it. She spent a weekend painting just for her own pleasure and it is one of my most prized gifts.

• Remember that the opposites of growth are sameness and death. Thus, you can resolve to live each day in a new way, being spontaneous and alive, or you can fear the unknown and remain the same—psychologically dead.

• Have a talk with those people in your life who you feel are most responsible for your fear of the unknown. State in no uncertain terms that you intend to do new things, and check out their reactions. You may find that their incredulity is one of the things that you've always worried about in the past, and as a result you chose immobilization over those disapproving looks. Now that you can handle the looks, state your Declaration of Independence from their control.

• Instead of "Do your best in everything" as a credo for you and your children, try "Select the things that are important to you, and work hard at them, and in the rest of your life, just do." It's O.K. not to do your best! In fact, the whole "Do your Best," syndrome is a myth. You never do your absolute best, nor does anyone else. There is always room for improvement, since perfection is not a human attribute.

• Don't let your convictions keep you stagnant. Believing something out of past experience and hanging on to that belief is an avoidance of reality. There is only what is now, and the truth of the present may not be the truth of the past. Assess your behavior not on what you believe, but in terms of what is and what you experience in the present. By allowing yourself to experience, rather than coloring your reality with beliefs, you'll find the unknown a fantastic place to be.

• Remember, nothing human is alien to you. You can be anything you choose. Imprint this on your mind and remind yourself of it when you fall into your typically safe evasive behavior.

• Become aware of avoiding the unknown as you are doing it. At that moment begin a dialogue with yourself. Tell yourself it's O.K. if you don't know where you are going at every moment of your life. Awareness of routine is the first step in changing it.

• Deliberately fail at something. Are you really less

of a person for losing a tennis game or painting a bad picture or are you still a worthwhile individual who just enjoyed some pleasant activity?

• Have a conversation with a member of a group that you've avoided in the past. You'll soon discover that your prejudices, when challenged by you, are keeping you stagnant and uninteresting. If you pre-judge anyone, you prevent yourself from dealing with them honestly since your viewpoint has already been established. The more different kinds of people you encounter, the more likely you are to remark to yourself how much you've been missing, and how foolish your fears have been. With these insights, the unknown will become an area for ever-increasing exploration rather than something to shun.

Some Final Thoughts on Fearing the Unknown

The above suggestions represent some constructive means of fighting fear of the unknown. The whole process begins with new insights into your avoidance behavior, followed by actively challenging the old behavior and moving in new directions. Just imagine if the great inventors or explorers of the past had feared the unknown. The entire population of the world would still reside in the Tigris-Euphrates Valley. The unknown is where growth resides. Both for civilization and for the individual.

Think of a road with a fork in it. In one direction lies security, in the other the great uncharted unknown. Which road would you take?

Robert Frost answered the question in *The Road Not Taken*.

> Two roads diverged in a wood, and I—
> I took the one less traveled by,
> And that has made all the difference.

The choice is yours. Your erroneous zone of fear of the unknown is waiting to be replaced by new exciting activities that will bring pleasure to your life. You don't have to know where you're going—as long as you're on your way.

VII
Breaking the Barrier
of Convention

There are no rules, laws or traditions that apply
universally . . . including this one.

The world is full of "shoulds" that people apply to
their behavior without evaluation, and the total of these
shoulds makes up a very large erroneous zone. You
may be guided by a set of rules and principles to which
you don't even subscribe, and yet you are unable to
break away and decide for yourself what works and
doesn't work for you.

Nothing is absolute. There are no rules or laws which
always make sense or provide the greatest amount of
good for all occasions. Flexibility is a far greater virtue,
and yet you may find it difficult, indeed impossible, to
break an unserviceable law or violate absurd tradition.
Fitting into your society or enculturation may be useful
for getting along at times, but carried to an extreme,
it can become a neurosis, particularly when unhappiness, depression and anxiety are the consequences of
your meeting the shoulds.

Nowhere is it being inferred or in any way suggested that you become contemptuous of the law, or
break rules simply because you see fit to do so. Laws
are necessary, and order is an important part of civilized
society. But blind adherence to convention is something
else entirely, something, in fact, which may be far more
destructive to the individual than violation of the rules.

Often rules are foolish, and traditions no longer make any sense. When this is the case, and you are unable to function effectively because you must follow senseless rules, that is the time to reconsider the rules and your behavior.

As Abraham Lincoln once put it, "I never had a policy that I could always apply. I've simply attempted to do what made the greatest amount of sense at the moment." He was not a slave to a single policy that had to apply in every single case, even if the policy was written with such an intention.

A should is unhealthy only when it gets in the way of healthy and effective behavior. If you find yourself doing annoying or otherwise counterproductive things which are the result of a should, you have renounced your freedom of choice and are allowing yourself to be controlled by some external force. A closer examination of this internal versus external control of yourself will be helpful before continuing to look at these erroneous musts which may clutter your life.

Internal vs. External Locus of Control

It has been estimated that a full seventy-five percent of the people in our culture are more external than internal in their personality orientation. This means that the chances are that you fit into this category more often than you don't. What does it mean to be "external" in your locus of control? Essentially, you are external if you assign responsibility for your emotional state in your present moments to someone or something external to yourself. Thus, if you were to be asked the question, "Why do you feel bad?" and you responded with answers like . . . "My parents mistreat me," "She hurt my feelings," "My friends don't like me," "My luck is down," or "Things just aren't going well," you would be in this external category. Conversely, if you were asked why you are so happy, and you responded: "My friends treat me well," "My luck has changed," "Nobody is bugging me," or "She came through for me," you are still in the external frame, assigning responsibility for how you feel to someone or something outside of you.

The internal locus of control person puts the responsibility for how he feels squarely on his own shoulders, and this person is indeed rare in our culture. When asked the same questions, he responds with internally oriented answers such as: "I tell myself the wrong things," "I put too much emphasis on what others say," "I worry about what someone else thinks," "I'm not strong enough now to avoid being unhappy," and "I don't have the skills to keep me from being miserable." Similarly, when the internally-put-together person is up, he responds with "I" references such as "I worked hard at being happy," "I made things work for me," "I'm telling myself the right things," "I'm in charge of me, and this is where I choose to be." Thus, you have one-fourth of the people taking responsibility for their own feelings, and three-fourths bestowing blame on external sources. Where do you fit in? Virtually all shoulds and traditions are imposed by external sources. That is, they come from someone or something outside of yourself. If you are loaded with shoulds and unable to break conventions which are prescribed by others, then you are in the external bag.

An excellent example of this externally directed kind of thinking is a client who came to me recently. We'll call her Barbara. Her major grievance was an obesity problem, but she had a host of minor complaints as well. When we started to discuss her weight problem, she said that she had always been overweight because she had a metabolism problem and also because her mother had forced food on her as a child. Her pattern of overeating continued now, she said, because her husband had neglected her and her children were inconsiderate of her. She had tried everything, she lamented —Weight Watchers, pills, a variety of diet doctors, even astrology. Therapy was to be her last resort. If I couldn't make her lose weight, she said, no one could.

As Barbara told her story—and viewed her own dilemma—it was no wonder she couldn't lose those unwanted pounds. Everything and everybody was conspiring against her—her mother, her husband, her children, even her own body and the stars. Weight Watchers and diet doctors might be able to help less afflicted souls but in Barbara's case the odds against her were too great.

Barbara was a classic example of external thinking. It was her mother, her husband, her children and some uncontrollable part of her own body that made her fat. It had nothing to do with her own choices to eat, or overeat, certain foods at certain times. Moreover, her attempts to alleviate her situation were as externally directed as her perceptions of the problem itself. Instead of recognizing that she had chosen to overeat in the past and she would have to learn to make new choices if she wanted to lose weight, Barbara turned to other people and things—society's accepted conventions for weight loss. When all her friends went to Weight Watchers, Barbara went. Each time a friend discovered a new diet doctor, Barbara was close on her heels for help.

After several weeks of counseling, Barbara began to recognize that her unhappiness and her complaints were the result of her own choices, not the actions of others. It began with an admission that she simply ate too much, often more than she really wanted, and did not exercise enough. Her first decision was to change her eating habits through sheer self-discipline. She could and would manipulate her own mind. Next time she felt hungry she resolved to reward herself with thoughts of her own internal strength rather than a cookie. Instead of blaming her husband and children for treating her badly and driving her to food, she began to see that she had been playing the martyr for years, virtually begging them to exploit her. Once Barbara began demanding to be treated well, she found that her family was only too ready to treat her that way, and instead of seeking solace in food she found fulfillment in relationships based on mutual respect and love.

Barbara even decided to spend less time with her mother whom she had come to see as running her life and ruining it with overdoses of food. Once Barbara came to recognize that her mother did not control her and that she could see her when she chose to, not when her mother said she should, and similarly that she didn't have to eat that piece of chocolate cake just because her mother said she should, Barbara began to enjoy rather than resent the time they spent together.

Finally Barbara realized that therapy had nothing to do with anything outside herself. I couldn't change her. She had to change herself. It took time, but gradually, with effort, Barbara replaced her external shoulds with internal standards of her own. She is now not only thinner, but happier as well. She knows that it isn't her husband or her children, her mother or the stars that are making her happy. She knows it is herself, for now she controls her own mind.

Fatalists, determinists and people who believe in luck are in the external slot. If you believe that your life is mapped out for you in advance, and you need only follow the appropriate roads, then you are very likely loaded with all of the shoulds that will keep you on your road map.

You can never find self-fulfillment if you persist in permitting yourself to be controlled by external forces or persist in thinking that you are controlled by external forces. Being effective does not mean eliminating all of the problems in your life. It does mean moving your locus of control from the external to the internal. In that way you make yourself responsible for everything that you experience emotionally. You are not a robot, running your life through a maze, filled up with other people's rules and regulations that don't even make sense to you. You can take a sterner look at the "rules" and begin to exercise some internal control over your own thinking, feeling and behavior.

BLAMING AND HERO WORSHIP: OPPOSITE ENDS OF THE SAME EXTERNALLY DIRECTED BEHAVIOR

Blame is a neat little device that you can use whenever you don't want to take responsibility for something in your life. It is the refuge of the externally oriented person.

All blame is a waste of time. No matter how much fault you find with another, and regardless of how much you blame him, it will not change you. The only thing blame does is keep the focus off you when you are looking for external reasons to explain your unhappiness or frustration. But blame itself is an act of folly. Even if blame has some effect, it will not be on you. You may succeed in making another feel guilty for something by blaming him, but you won't succeed in changing whatever it is about you that is making you unhappy. You may succeed in not thinking about it; but you won't succeed in changing it.

The tendency to focus on others can go to the opposite extreme where it surfaces as hero worship. In this case you may find yourself looking to others to determine your values. If so-and-so does it, then I should do it too. Hero worship is a form of self-repudiation. It makes others more important than you, and relates your own fulfillment to something outside of yourself. While there is nothing self-defeating about appreciating others and their accomplishments, it becomes an erroneous zone when you model your own behavior on their standards.

All of your heroes are people. They are all human. They do the same things that you do every day. They itch where you itch, they have bad breath in the morning just like you. (The only good hero is a ham and cheese or possibly an eggplant parmigiana.) All are wasteful of your efforts.

All the great heroes of your life have taught you nothing. And they are no better than you, in any way. Politicians, actors, athletes, rock-stars, your boss, therapist, teacher, spouse, or whoever, are just skillful at what they do—nothing more. And if you make them your heroes and elevate them to positions above yourself, then you are into that external bag of giving others the responsibility for your good feelings.

If you blame at one end or hero worship at the other, you are someplace on this Focusing On Others Line.

Hero Worship

Blame   The F.O.O.L.

You are behaving as a fool if you look outside of you for an explanation of how you should feel or what you should do. Taking credit as well as responsibility for yourself is the first step to eliminating this erroneous zone. Be your own hero. When you get out of the blaming and hero worship behavior you'll be moving over from the external to the internal side of the ledger. And on the internal side there are no universal shoulds, either for yourself or for others.

The Right vs. Wrong Trap

The question of right vs. wrong as it applies here has nothing to do with religious, philosophical or moral issues of *a priori* rightness or wrongness. That is a discussion for another place. Here the subject is you, and how your notions of right and wrong get in the way of your own happiness. Your rights and wrongs are your universal shoulds. You may have adopted some unhealthy stances which include right means good or just, while wrong is equated with bad or unjust. This is nonsense. Rights and wrongs in this sense do not exist. The word right implies a guarantee that if you do something a certain way, you'll have sure-fire results. But there are no guarantees. You can begin to think in terms of any decision as bringing about something different, or more effective, or legal, but the moment it becomes a question of right vs. wrong, you are trapped into the "I've always got to be right and when things or people are not right, then I'm going to be unhappy" trap.

Perhaps some of your need to find the right answer has to do with the search for certainty that was discussed in the chapter on fear of the unknown. This may be a part of your tendency to dichotomize, or to divide the world neatly into extremes such as black/white, yes/no, good/bad and right/wrong. Few things fit neatly into those categories and most intelligent folks roam around in those gray areas, rarely coming to rest on either black or white. This proclivity for being right is most clearly evidenced in marriage and other adult relationships. Discussions inevitably become a contest which results in one partner being right, and the other wrong. You hear it all the time. "You always think you're right," and "You'll never admit you're wrong." But there is no right and wrong here. People are different and they see things from different perspectives. If one must be right, then a breakdown in communication is the only predictable outcome.

The only way out of this trap is to stop thinking in those erroneous right vs. wrong ways. As I explained to Clifford, who was in a marriage in which he argued every day about every conceivable topic, "Instead of attempting to convince your wife how wrong she is, why not simply have discussions in which you have no should-expectations for her. As long as she is allowed to be different from you, you'll eliminate the incessant arguing in which you doggedly, albeit frustratedly, pursue being right." Clifford was able to set aside this neurotic need, and also to put some communication and love back in his marriage. All rights and wrongs of every description represent shoulds of one kind or another. And the shoulds get in your way, particularly when they conflict with another person's need to have his own as well.

Indecisiveness as a Spin-Off of Right vs. Wrong Thinking

I once asked a client if he had trouble making a decision, and he said, "Well—Yes and No." Perhaps you have difficulty with decision-making, even with small things. This is a direct outgrowth of the inclination to divide things into right and wrong categories. The indecision comes from wanting to be right, and the postponement of a choice keeps you from dealing with the anxiety that you choose for yourself whenever you feel you've been wrong. Once you take away the rightness and wrongness of every decision (because right implies a guarantee), then decision-making will become a snap. If you are trying to decide on the right college to attend, you might stay immobilized forever, even after you've made the decision, because maybe it wasn't right. Instead, shift the process to, "There is no such thing as the right college. If I select A then these are the more likely consequences, while B will probably bring about these." Neither is right, one is simply different than the other, and you'll have no guarantees regardless of the choice to attend, A, B, or Z. Similarly you can ease your indecision-neurosis by viewing all potential outcomes as being neither right nor wrong, good nor bad, even better or worse. Simply different. If you buy this dress which you like, this is how you are going to look, which is only different from (not better than) wearing that dress. Once you give up those inaccurate and self-destructive rights and wrongs, you'll find decision-making a simple matter of weighing which consequences you'd prefer at a given present moment. And if you begin to choose regret over the decision, rather than deciding that regret is a waste of your time (because it keeps you living in the past), you'll simply resolve to make a different decision in your next present moment, one that will bring consequences that the earlier decision failed to bring. But never attempting to put it into a right or wrong categorization.

Nothing is more important than anything else. The child collecting seashells is not doing something more right or wrong than the President of General Motors making a major corporate decision. They are different. Nothing more!

You may believe that wrong ideas are bad and should not be stated, while right ideas are to be encouraged. Perhaps with your children, friends or spouse, you say, "It's not worth saying or doing, if it's not said or done right." But danger lurks here. This authoritarian stance will lead to totalitarianism when extended to national and international proportions. Who decides the rightness? That is the question that can never be answered satisfactorily. The law doesn't decide if it's wrong, only if it's legal. More than a century ago, John Stuart Mill, writing in *On Liberty*, proclaimed:

> We can never be sure that the opinion we are endeavoring to stifle is false opinion, and if we were sure, stifling it would be an evil still.

Your effectiveness is not measured by your ability to make a right choice. How you handle yourself emotionally after any choice is a far greater barometer of your personal present-moment togetherness, since a right choice represents those shoulds that you are working at eliminating. New thinking will be helpful on two counts —one, you'll banish those senseless shoulds and become more internal, and two, you'll find decision-making less troublesome without those erroneous right and wrong categories.

The Folly of Shoulds, Musts and Oughts

There is a neat little word, coined by Albert Ellis, for the tendency to incorporate shoulds into your life. It is "musterbation." You are "musterbating" whenever you find yourself behaving in ways that you feel you must, even though you might prefer some other form of behavior. Karen Horney, the brilliant psychiatrist, has devoted an entire chapter of *Neurosis and Human Growth* to this topic, and she titles it, "The Tyranny of the Should." She comments:

> The shoulds always produce a feeling of strain, which is all the greater the more a person tries to actualize his shoulds in his behavior. . . . Furthermore, because of externalizations, the shoulds always contribute to *disturbance in human relations* in one way or another.*

Do shoulds determine much of your life? Do you feel you should be kind to your colleagues, supportive of your spouse, helpful to your children and always work hard? And if at any time you fail in one of these shoulds do you berate yourself and hence take on that strain and disturbance to which Karen Horney alludes above? But perhaps these are not your shoulds. If, in fact, they belong to others and you have merely borrowed them, then you are musterbating.

There are just as many should-nots as there are shoulds. These include: you should not be rude, angry, foolish, silly, juvenile, lewd, gloomy, offensive and scores of others. But you don't have to musterbate. Ever. It's all right to be lacking in composure, or to not understand. You're allowed to be undignified if you choose to. No one is keeping score on you, or going to punish you for not being something that someone else said you must be. Besides, you can never be anything that you don't want to be all of the time. It's just not possible. Therefore, any should will have to produce strain in you, since you won't be able to fulfill your erroneous expectation. The strain does not result from your undignified, nonsupportive, indiscreet or whatever behavior, but from the imposition of the should.

* Karen Horney, *Neurosis and Human Growth* (New York: W. W. Norton & Co., 1950), p. 81.

Etiquette as a Should

Etiquette is a beautiful example of useless and unhealthy enculturation. Think of all the little meaningless rules you've been encouraged to adopt simply because Emily Post, Amy Vanderbilt, or Abigail van Buren has so written. Eat your corn on the cob this way, always wait for the hostess to start before eating, introduce the man to the woman, sit on that side of the church at a wedding, tip this, wear that, use these words. Don't consult yourself; look it up in the book. While good manners are certainly appropriate—they simply entail consideration for other people—about ninety percent of all the etiquette guidelines are meaningless rules that were composed arbitrarily at one time. There is no proper way for you; there is only what you decide is right for you—as long as you don't make it hard for others to get along. You can choose how you'll introduce people, what you'll tip, what you'll wear, how you'll speak, where you'll sit, how you'll eat, and so on, strictly on the basis of what you want. Anytime you fall into the trap of "What *should* I wear," or "How *should* I do it," you're giving up a chunk of yourself. I'm not making a case here for being a social rebel since that would be a form of approval-seeking through nonconformity, but rather this is a plea for being self- rather than other-directed in the everyday running of your life. Being true to yourself means being devoid of the need for an external support system.

Blind Obedience to Rules and Laws

Some of the most despicable human behavior ever recorded was done under the guise of following orders. The Nazis executed six million Jews and murdered and mistreated countless millions of others because it was the "Law." Later, after the war, responsibility for these acts of barbarism was shifted rapidly up the hierarchy of Nazi power until throughout Germany the only people who could be held accountable for these heinous crimes were Hitler and his chief henchmen. Everyone else was merely following orders and the law of the Third Reich.

In Suffolk County, New York, a county spokesman recently explained why people who had been inadvertently overcharged on their real estate taxes could not be reimbursed. "The law says that past tax bills cannot be reevaluated once they are paid. It's the law, I can't help it. My job is to enforce it, not to interpret it." Indeed, in another time and another place, he'd have made an excellent executioner. But you know this refrain. You hear it every day. Don't think, just obey the rules, even if they are absurd.

At swimming pools, tennis courts and other public places, about half of the rules make no sense. Recently one hot evening I asked a group of young people sitting around a pool, obviously thirsting to get in, why they were lounging near the edge, when the pool was empty. They responded that it was for adults between 6:00 and 8:00 P.M. This was the rule, and despite the fact that no adults wanted to use it, the rule was still being enforced. No flexibility, no ability to alter the rule when circumstances so warrant, simply blind obedience to a rule that had no logical reason at that moment. When I encouraged them to see about shifting the rules, I received a phone call from the management telling me that I was promoting insurrection.

One of the best examples of blind adherence to the rules—no matter how silly they may be—can be found in the military. A colleague of mine tells of an excellent example of this obedience mentality. When stationed on Guam, in the South Pacific, he was struck by the willingness of many enlisted men to enforce rules that were obviously absurd. Officers were permitted to sit on the red benches which were sheltered and watch the outdoor movies. At the midnight showing of the movie, which officers never attended, there was an enlisted man

assigned to ensure that no one sat on the red benches.
Thus, each evening you would see a group of enlisted
sailors sitting in the rain, with one of their own ranks
guarding a section of empty red benches, to ensure that
the rule was followed. When my colleague inquired why
such an absurd policy was being enforced, he was given
the standard answer, "I don't make the rules, I just
enforce them."

Herman Hesse said in *Demian,*

> Those who are too lazy and comfortable to think
> for themselves and be their own judges obey the
> laws. Others sense their own laws within them;
> things are forbidden to them that every honorable
> man will do any day in the year and other things
> are allowed to them that are generally despised.
> Each person must stand on his own feet.*

If you must comply with all the rules all the time, you
are destined to a life of emotional servitude. But our
culture teaches that it is naughty to disobey, that you
shouldn't do anything that is against the rules. The
important thing is to determine for yourself which rules
work, and are necessary to preserve order in our culture and which can be broken without harm to yourself
or others. There is no percentage in rebelling just for
the sake of rebelling, but there are great rewards in
being your own person and living your life according
to your own standards.

Resisting Enculturation and Traditions When They Affect You Negatively

Progress, yours personally and the world's, depends
on unreasonable men, rather than people who adapt
to their society and accept whatever comes along. Progress depends on individuals who are innovators, who

* Hermann Hesse, *Demian* (New York: Bantam Books, 1974), p. 53.

reject convention and fashion their own worlds. In order to shift from coping to doing, you'll have to learn to resist enculturation and the many pressures to conform. To function fully, a resistance to enculturation is almost a given. You may be viewed by some as insubordinate, which is the price you'll pay for thinking for yourself. You may be seen as different, be labeled selfish or rebellious, incur disapproval from many "normal" people, and at times be ostracized. Some people will not take kindly to your resistance to norms they've adopted for themselves. You'll hear the old argument of, "What if everybody decided to obey only the rules they wanted to? What kind of a society would we have then?" The simple answer to this, of course, is that everybody won't! Most people's addiction to external supports and shoulds prohibits such a stand.

What we're talking about here has nothing to do with anarchy. No one wants to destroy society, but many of us would like to give the individual more freedom within it, freedom from meaningless musts and silly shoulds.

Even sensible laws and rules will not apply under every set of circumstances. What we are striving for is choice, that is, the ability to be free from the servant mentality of constant adherence to the shoulds. You do not have to be always as your culture expects you to be. If you are, and feel an inability to be otherwise, you are indeed a follower, one of a flock who allows others to determine his course. Leading your own life involves flexibility and repeated personal assessments of how well the rule works at a particular present moment. True, it's often easier to follow, to blindly do as you're told, but once you recognize that the law is there to serve you, not to make you a servant, you can begin to eliminate the musterbation behavior.

If you're going to learn to resist enculturation, you'll have to become a shrugger. Others will still choose to obey even if it hurts them, and you will have to learn to allow them their choice. No anger, only your own convictions. A colleague of mine was in the Navy, stationed aboard an aircraft carrier home ported in San Francisco at the time President Eisenhower was visiting northern California on a political swing. They were commanded to spell out in human formation the words, HI IKE, so that the President could look down from his helicopter and view the message. My friend decided the idea was insane, and decided not to do it, because it conflicted with everything he stood for. But rather than stage a revolt, he simply slipped away for the afternoon, and allowed everyone else to participate in this demeaning ritual. He passed up his one chance to dot the i in Hi. No put-down of those who chose otherwise, no useless fighting, simply shrugging and letting others go their own way.

Resisting enculturation means making decisions for yourself and carrying them out as efficiently and quietly as possible. No bandwagons or hostile demonstrations where they will do no good. The foolish rules, traditions and policies will never go away, but you don't have to be a part of them. Just shrug as others go through their sheep motions. If they want to behave that way, fine for them but that's not for you. To make a big fuss is almost always the surest way to incur wrath and create more obstacles for yourself. You'll find scores of everyday occurrences where it is easier to circumvent the rules quietly than to start a protest movement. You can decide to be the person you want to be, or the one others want you to be. It's up to you.

Virtually all new ideas which have resulted in change in our society were at one time scorned, and many of them were illegal as well. All progress involves flying in the face of old rules that no longer apply. People ridiculed the Edisons, Henry Fords, Einsteins, and Wright Brothers—until they were successful. You will meet with contempt, too, as you begin to resist meaningless policies.

Some Typical Should Behaviors

The roll of "have-to" behaviors could fill an entire book. Here is a sampling of the more common examples of these actions as they surface in our culture.

• Believing that there is a place for everything and everything must be in its place. The organization syndrome means you are uncomfortable if things aren't in their designated locations.

• Asking "What should I wear" on a regular basis, as if there were only one acceptable mode of dressing and it is determined by other people. White pants and pastel colors are *only* worn in the summer. Wool is *always* a winter fabric, and other similar "being controlled by the seasons" *musts* that infiltrate your life. (In *Hawaii*, James Michener describes the New Englanders who arrived in the tropical climate of Hawaii, and when October arrived, even though it was still eighty-five degrees, they habitually trotted out their winter clothes and dressed uncomfortably for six months . . . Why? Because they were supposed to.) Being a slave to the dictates of fashion critics, and wearing only "What's in" because, after all, you *have to* fit in.

• Assuming that certain drinks must go with certain food. White wine must accompany fish and fowl. Red wine goes only with beef. Being locked into somebody's rules on what to eat with what.

• Shifting blame for your actions to others. "It's really her fault, she made us late." "Don't blame me, he's the one who did it."

• You must go to a wedding or send a gift, even if you don't like them. You just don't ignore invitations even when you want to. You may feel resentful about buying the gift, but go through the motions anyhow because that's the way things are supposed to be done. Conversely, attending funerals that you'd rather not go to, but do because you're supposed to. You must attend such formal functions to show that you grieve or respect or have the appropriate emotions.

• Attending religious services which you dislike and don't believe in because it is expected of you and you want to do the right thing.

• Giving titles to those who serve you, which elevates them by implication to a position higher than you. What do you call your dentist? If it's doctor, is it really just a vocational title? Do you say Carpenter Jones, or Plumber Smith? If it is out of respect for his position, what makes you think his position is loftier than yours? If he is paid to serve you, why is it that he gets a title and you get called by your name?

• Going to bed when it gets to be bedtime, rather than when you're tired.

• Having sex only one or two ways because those are the only acceptable ways, or only participating in sexual activities when all conditions are met, such as, the kids are asleep, you are not tired, it's dark in the room, you're in your own bed, and on and on.

• Selecting roles in daily living because the culture demands it. Women do the dishes, men take out the garbage. Housework is for the wife, outdoor work is for the husband. Boys do this, girls do that.

• Obedience to silly household rules and traditions that don't work for your family, such as asking permission to leave the table, everyone eating at the same time when it is more inconvenient to do it that way or bedtimes that are without rationale.

• Following the dictates of all signs whether they make sense or not. No Talking! No Entry! No anything! Never challenging a sign, or even assuming that it doesn't belong there in the first place. People make signs and people also make mistakes.

• Keeping mattress tags on for years because they say do not remove under penalty of law.

• Always having Sunday dinner at Mama's, although you'd rather not. After all, it is a tradition, and even if everyone doesn't like it, including Mama, you must preserve tradition.

• When reading a book, always starting at page one and reading every word to the end, even if half of it doesn't apply. Finishing a book you don't like because you're halfway through it, and, if you've read half, you must read it all.

• Women never asking men for dates. After all, that's the male's role. Or never initiating a telephone call, or opening the door for a man, or paying the bill, or countless other absurd traditions that serve no real purpose.

• Sending out holiday greeting cards and resenting them. Doing so because you've always done it, and it is expected of you.

• Striving for grades in school or forcing your children to do so. Learning not for your own satisfaction but for the symbols that will eventually appear on the transcript.

• Always asking: "Is he/she right for me?" and being regularly perplexed in search of the right person.

• Going everywhere with your partner because it is expected, even though you both would prefer to be in different places at that particular time.

• Consulting a "how-to" book for everything, because every job must be done a certain way. Not being able to differentiate between manuals that impart useful information and those that merely tell you how things ought to be.

• Is this the right dress, hat, automobile, furniture, salad dressing, appetizer, book, college, job, etc. Being anxious over the search for the right item and as a result being in that indecision and doubt bag.

• Making rewards, plaques, titles, honors and all merit badges more important than your own evaluation of your achievements.

• Saying, "I could never be as great as———"

• Applauding in an audience when you didn't like the performance.

• Tipping for poor service.

• Sports-fan behavior in which you go crazy over a home team victory or loss, and live vicariously through the accomplishments or lack of accomplishments of athletes.

A Look at the Common Payoffs of Musterbation

Some of the reasons you have for hanging on to your shoulds are detailed below. These payoffs, like those in all erroneous zones, are mostly self-destructive but nevertheless constitute a certain support system of their own.

• You can take solace in being a "good boy" or a "good girl" by following all of your shoulds. You can pat yourself on the back for being obedient. This dividend is a regressive one in which you go back to an earlier developmental period when you were rewarded with approval whenever you behaved, which meant relying on someone else to establish your rules of conduct.

• Your obedience to the external should allows you to assign the responsibility for your standing still to the should rather than to yourself. As long as the should is the rationale for what you are (or aren't), you can avoid the risks involved in trusting yourself to change. Thus your shoulds keep you from growing. For example, Marjorie has a should in her head that all premarital sex is a taboo. She is thirty-four years old, and to date she has never had a sexual experience because of this learned should. But Marjorie has no inner peace. She would like to have a sexual relationship, and she is very much dissatisfied with herself in this area. Moreover, it is possible that Marjorie will never get married, and her should (in this case should-not) would then keep her from participating in sex for an entire lifetime. When she is confronted with this possibility she shudders at the thought, and yet her should-not is still there. Marjorie has spillover effects from her should. She can't even stay overnight in the same house with her boyfriend out of fear of being judged by others. Thus she is constantly being inconvenienced because of her shoulds by having to come home to Mama at night. Hanging on to them keeps her from the risky business of testing herself out in the scary act of sexual involvement. But her response is always, "I shouldn't do it." Plainly, her shoulds work against her own happiness.

• Your musts make it possible for you to maneuver others. By telling someone this is the way it should be done, you can make him do it the way you want it to be done.

• It is easier to haul out a should when you lack confidence in yourself. As your self-image wanes, the should becomes your bulwark.

• You can remain self-righteous about your behavior and retain your hostility when others don't fit into the shoulds that you have for yourself and the rest of the world. Hence, you build yourself up in your mind at the expense of others who don't obey the rule-patterns.

• You can win approval by conforming. You feel good by fitting-in, which is what you were told all along that you *should* be doing. That old approval-seeking need creeps in here as well.

• As long as you focus on others, and live through their successes and failures, you don't have to work on yourself. Having heroes can reinforce your own low opinion of yourself and allow you to escape from having to work on yourself. As long as the heroes can be the cause of your good feelings, or responsible for your bad feelings, there is no reason for you to take on that responsibility. Your self-worth in this case is really other-worth and thus fleeting and transitory. It depends upon all of those great people, and how they come through for you.

Some Strategies for Removing Some of Your Shoulds

Basically your chore in scrubbing up this zone involves risk-taking. Doing! Resolving to be different than the way you've been taught is proper when that way doesn't work for you. Here are some tactics that will be helpful in getting out of your musterbatory habits.

• Begin with insight into your own behavior. Study the neurotic dividends spelled out above. Then ask yourself why you are burdening yourself with so many shoulds. Ask yourself if you really believe in them, or if you've just become accustomed to behaving that way.

• List all of the rules you abide by, which just don't seem to apply. Those stupid conventional behaviors that you complain about, but can't seem to shed. Then, make your own "Rules of Conduct" that make the greatest amount of sense to you. Write them down, even if you don't believe at this time that you are capable of living them out.

• Start your own traditions. For example, if you've always decorated your Christmas Tree on Christmas Eve, and you'd rather do it three days before, begin a new Christmas tradition—one that makes sense to you.

• Have a consultation with your relatives and friends about the many rules of conduct you all follow which you find distasteful. Perhaps you'll be able to bring about some new rules which appear to be more reasonable to everyone. You'll discover that the old rules are still in effect only because no one ever seriously thought to challenge them in the past.

• Keep an internal/external journal. Write down your "external" references in which you assign responsibility to others for how you are feeling. See if you can shift yourself to the "internal" side with some new acts of courage. Keep track of your success in moving over to the internal side.

• See how many rules you impose on others. Ask them if they really need those directives, or if they would behave in the identical fashion without them. Perhaps you'll even learn that they could come up with more effective and flexible guidelines.

• Take a risk on challenging a rule or policy that you'd like to eliminate. But be prepared to deal without hostility with the consequences of your behavior. For example if you've always believed that a woman shouldn't ask a man for a date and you find yourself without a date on a weekend, call up a man and see what happens. Or, take back a defective garment even if the rule is *no refunds*, and effectively challenge the policy, vowing to go to the top if necessary. Don't be guided by the policies of others which have you being a victim as the final result.

• Think of decisions as having different consequences, rather than as being right or wrong. In making decisions, eliminate the notion of right and wrong and say either one is okay, and each will bring about different consequences. Trust yourself to make the decision rather than relying on some external kind of guarantee. Please yourself instead of meeting an outside standard.

• Try to live in your present moments and make your rules and shoulds apply only for that time. Rather than assuming them to be universals, recognize them as applicable only at this moment.

• Refuse to share your rule-breaking behavior with anyone. It is only for you, and you don't want to get into an approval-seeking posture, in which the reason for resisting enculturation is to win attention and therefore adulation.

• Get rid of the roles that you (and others) are assuming in your life. Be whatever you want to be, rather than what you think you are supposed to be because you are a man, woman, middle-aged, or whatever.

• Refuse for a given segment of a conversation to focus on others. Practice in ever-increasing time periods not projecting blame, or talking about another person, event, or idea in a complaining or fault-finding manner.

• Stop waiting for others to change. Ask yourself why others should be different simply because you would like it better if they were. Recognize that every person has a right to be whatever they choose, even if you irritate yourself about it.

• Come up with a blame list, wherein you detail

everything about yourself that you dislike. It can look something like this:

What I Dislike About Me and My Life	Who, What Is To Blame
I'm too fat	Sara Lee, metabolism, mother, McDonald's heredity
I have poor eyesight	Parents, grandparents, God, genetics, homework, Con-Ed
I'm lousy in mathematics ...:.....	Elementary teachers, sister, deficient math genes, mother
I have no boy/girl friends	Luck, all creeps at my school, parents, I can't wear makeup
I'm too tall	Genetics, God, mother
I'm unhappy	The economy, Dow-Jones, divorce, my children hate me, illness
My breasts are too small	Mother, genetics, luck, no early nourishment, God, Satan
My hair is the wrong color	Helena Rubenstein, heredity, girl friend, the sun
The state of the world bugs me	Presidents Ford, Nixon, Johnson, etc., the Communists, humanity
My neighbors are bitchy	The neighborhood, "Those kinds of people," zoning regulations
My tennis outcome	The wind, the sun, the net is too high/low,

	the distractions, my cramps, my sore arm, leg, etc.
I don't feel well	My metabolism, my period, my doctor, the food, the heat, the cold, the wind, the rain, the pollen, You Name It.

Now add up your total blame score and see if you are any different now that you have fault and blame appropriately doled out to all of the precise people and things that are responsible for your feelings. Isn't that something? You are exactly the same. Whether you blame or don't, you stay as you are unless you *do* something constructive to correct your dislikes. You can use this as an exercise in seeing the futility of blaming.

• Announce out loud that you just blamed and that you are working on eliminating this behavior. By stating it as a goal, you'll be mindful of your proclivities in this direction.

• Decide that any and all unhappiness that you choose will never be the result of someone else, but rather that it will be the result of you and your own behavior. Remind yourself constantly that any externally caused unhappiness reinforces your own slavery, since it assumes that you have no control over yourself or them, but they have control over you.

• When someone is blaming, politely ask them, "Would you like to know if I want to hear what you are telling me right now?" That is, teach others not to use you as a blame receptacle and begin to label other people's blaming and fault-finding so that you get in touch with recognizing it in yourself. You can label it with a nonoffensive treatment such as, "You just made George responsible for how you feel. Do you really think it's that way?" Or, "You keep saying that if only the market would go up, you'd be happier. You really give it a lot of control over your life." Your recognition of others' blames and shoulds will help you to eliminate such behavior in yourself.

• Refer back to the lists of shoulds discussed earlier in this chapter. Try to substitute some new and different behavior for these old habits—perhaps a late night dinner, or changing your sexual position, or wearing what you like. Begin to trust yourself and give less credence to those external musts.

• Remind yourself that what other people do is not what bothers you, it's your reaction to it. Instead of saying "They shouldn't do that," say, "I wonder why I bother myself with what they are doing."

Some Final Thoughts on Should Behavior

Ralph Waldo Emerson wrote in *Literary Ethics* in 1838,

> Men grind and grind in the mill of a truism, and nothing comes out but what was put in. But the moment they desert the tradition for a spontaneous thought, then poetry, wit, hope, virtue, learning, anecdote, all flock to their aid.

What a beautiful thought. Stay with tradition and you ensure that you'll always be the same, but toss it aside, and the world is yours to use as creatively as you choose.

Become your own judge of your conduct and learn to rely on yourself to make present-moment decisions. Cease leafing through a lifetime of policies and traditions for an answer. Sing your own song of happiness in any way that you choose, oblivious to how it is supposed to be.

VIII

The Justice Trap

If the world were so organized that everything had to be fair, no living creature could survive for a day. The birds would be forbidden to eat worms, and everyone's self-interest would have to be served.

We are conditioned to look for justice in life and when it doesn't appear, we tend to feel anger, anxiety or frustration. Actually, it would be equally productive to search for the fountain of youth, or some such myth. Justice does not exist. It never has, and it never will. The world is simply not put together that way. Robins eat worms. That's not fair to the worms. Spiders eat flies. That's not fair to the flies. Cougars kill coyotes. Coyotes kill badgers. Badgers kill mice. Mice kill bugs. Bugs . . . You have only to look at nature to realize there is no justice in the world. Tornadoes, floods, tidal waves, draughts are all unfair. It is a mythological concept, this justice business. The world and the people in it go on being unfair every day. You can choose to be happy or unhappy, but it has nothing to do with the lack of justice you see around you.

This is not a sour view of humanity and the world, but rather an accurate report of what that world is like. Justice is simply a concept that has almost no applicability, particularly as it pertains to your own choices about fulfillment and happiness. But too many of us tend to demand that fairness be an inherent part of our relations with others. "It isn't fair," "You have no right

to do that if I can't" and "Would *I* do that to you?"
These are the sentences that we use. We seek justice
and use the lack of it as a justification for unhappiness.
The demand for justice is not the neurotic behavior. It
only becomes an erroneous zone when you punish yourself with a negative emotion as you fail to see evidence
of the justice that you so futilely demand. In this case
the self-defeating behavior is not the demand for justice,
but the immobilization that may result from no-justice-
reality.

Our culture promises justice. Politicians refer to it in
all of their campaign speeches. "We need equality and
justice for all." Yet day after day, nay, century after
century, the lack of justice continues. Poverty, war,
pestilence, crime, prostitution, dope and murders persist generation after generation in public and private
life. And if the history of humanity can be used as a
guide they will continue.

Injustice is a constant, but you, in your infinite new
wisdom, can decide to fight that injustice and refuse to
be seduced into being emotionally immobilized over it.
You can work at helping to eradicate injustice, and you
can decide that you won't be psychologically defeated
by it.

The legal system promises justice. "The people demand justice," and some of them even work to make it
happen. But it generally doesn't. Those with money are
not convicted. Judges and policemen are often bought
by the powerful. A President and Vice-President of the
United States are pardoned or wrist-slapped for obvious
felonies. The poor fill the jails, and have next to no
chance of beating the system. It's not fair. But it's true.
Spiro Agnew becomes rich after evading his income
taxes. Richard Nixon is exonerated, and his yes-men
serve a few months in a minimum security prison, while
the poor and members of minority groups rot in jail
waiting for trial, waiting for a chance. A visit to any
local courthouse or police station will prove that the in-
fluential have a separate set of rules, although this is
relentlessly denied by the authorities. Where is the

justice? Nowhere! Your deciding to fight it may be admirable indeed, but your choosing to be upset by it is as neurotic as guilt, approval-seeking or any other of the self-flagellating behavior that constitutes your erroneous zones.

"It's Not Fair!" The Slogan of Ineffective Relationships

The demand for justice may infiltrate your personal relationships and prevent you from communicating effectively with others. The "It's not fair" slogan is one of the more common—and destructive—laments made by one person against another. In order for you to consider something unfair you must compare yourself to another individual or group of individuals. Your mindset goes something like this: "If they can do it, so can I." "It's not fair for you to have more than I." "But I didn't get to do that, why should you?" On and on they go. In this case you're determining what is good for you on the basis of someone else's conduct. They, not you, are in charge of your emotions. If you are upset because of not being able to do something that someone else has done, then you've given them control over you. Whenever you compare yourself to anyone else, you are playing the "It's not fair" game, and shifting from self-reliance to other-directed external thinking.

One of my clients, an attractive young woman named Judy, is a good example of this kind of self-destructive thinking. Judy complained about her unhappy marriage of five years. One night in counseling she acted out a marital argument for the group. When the young man who was taking the role of Judy's insurance salesman husband said something unpleasant to her, Judy immediately countered with "Why did you say that? I never say things like that to you." When he mentioned their two children, Judy said, "That isn't fair. I never bring the children into an argument." When their role working turned to a prospective evening's entertainment, Judy's reasoning was once again, "That isn't fair. You get out all the time while I have to stay home with the children."

Judy ran her marriage on a tally sheet. One for you, one for me. Everything must be fair. If I act this way, you must act the same way. It was no wonder she was hurt and resentful most of the time, more concerned with righting imaginary injustices than examining and perhaps improving her marriage.

Judy's search for justice was a neurotic dead end. She was assessing her husband's behavior on the basis of her own and her happiness on the basis of her husband's behavior. Were she to stop her incessant keeping track and begin going after the things she wants without having to be in debt to the other, then her relationship would improve significantly.

Fairness is an external concept—a way of avoiding the taking charge of your own life. Instead of thinking of anything as being unfair, you can decide what you really want, and then set about devising strategies for attaining it, independent of what anyone else in the world wants or does. The simple facts are that everyone is different, and no amount of your bitching about others having it better than you will bring about any positive self-changes. You'll need to eliminate the other-references, and throw away the binoculars that focus on what others are doing. Some people work less and get more money. Others get promoted out of favoritism, when you have the ability. Your spouse and children will continue to do things differently from you. But if you focus on yourself rather than compare yourself to others, then you will have no opportunity to upset yourself with the lack of equality you observe. The backdrop for virtually all neurosis is making others' behavior more significant than your own. If you carry around the "If he can do it, so should I" sentences, you'll be running your life on the basis of someone else and never create your own life.

Jealousy: A "Demand for Justice" Sideshow

John Dryden called jealousy "the jaundice of the soul." If your jealously gets in your way, and creates any amount of emotional immobility, then you can set as a goal the elimination of this wasteful thinking. Jealousy is really a demand that someone love you in a certain way, and you saying "It isn't fair" when they don't. It comes from a lack of self-confidence, simply because it is an other-directed activity. It allows their behavior to be the cause of your emotional discomfort. People who really like themselves don't choose jealousy or allow themselves to be distraught when someone else doesn't play fair.

You can never predict how someone you love will react to another human being, but if they choose to be affectionate or loving you can only experience the immobility of jealousy if you see their decisions as having anything to do with you. That is your choice. If a partner loves another, he isn't being "unfair," he is simply being. If you label it unfair, you'll probably end up trying to figure out why. A perfect example is a client of mine who was furious because her husband had an affair. She became obsessed with trying to figure out why. She was constantly asking, "Where did I go wrong?" "What's wrong with me?" "Wasn't I good enough for him?" and similar self-doubting questions. Helen was always thinking about the injustice of her husband's infidelity. She even contemplated having an affair herself as a way to right the balance. She cried a great deal and alternated between fury and sadness.

Helen's faulty thinking, which leads her to unhappiness, lies in her demand for justice which suffocates her in this relationship. She has made her husband's choice to engage in sex the reason for her to be upset. At the same time she is using his behavior as a rationale for doing something that she probably wanted to do for a long time—but didn't because it isn't fair. Helen's insistence on strict justice would have meant that if she were the first to have an affair, then her husband would have to retaliate. Helen's emotional condition will not improve until she decides that his decision was made independent of her, and that he might have a thousand reasons of his own, all unrelated to Helen, for his sexual exploration. Maybe he just wanted to do something different, perhaps he felt love for someone besides his wife, or perhaps he wanted to prove his virility or keep old age at bay. Whatever the reason, it has nothing to do with Helen. She can see the affair as something between two people rather than as something against her. The upset rests solely in Helen. She can continue to bruise herself with the self-flagellating jealousy in which she is less important than her husband or his mistress, or she can recognize that someone else's affair has nothing to do with her self-worth.

Some Typical "Demand for Justice" Behaviors

"Searching-for-equity" behavior is obvious in virtually all areas of life. If you are the least bit perceptive you'll see it cropping up over and over in yourself and others. Here are some of the more common examples of this kind of behavior.

- Complaining that others make more money for doing the same work.
- Saying it isn't fair that a Frank Sinatra, Sammy Davis, Barbra Streisand, Catfish Hunter or Joe Namath make the kind of salaries that they do, and being upset by it.
- Being upset that others get away with infractions, while you always get caught. From speeders on the highway to Nixon's pardon, you insist that justice *must* prevail.
- All of the "Would I treat you that way?" sentences in which the assumption is that everyone should be exactly like you.
- Always reciprocating when someone does a favor

for you. If you invite me for dinner, then I owe you one or at least a bottle of wine. This sort of behavior is often justified as good manners or politeness, but in reality it is simply a means of keeping the scales of justice in balance.

• Kissing someone back or saying "I love you, too" instead of accepting it and expressing your own feelings whenever you choose. The implication is that it isn't fair to have an "I love you" or kiss without giving one back.

• Having sex with someone out of obligation, even though you don't want to, because it really isn't fair not to be cooperative. Thus you operate by justice rather than what you would like to do at a particular present moment.

• Always insisting on things being consistent. Remember Emerson's often misquoted line:

A foolish consistency is the hobgoblin of little minds.

If you always want things to be the "right" way, you are in this "little-minds" category.

• In arguments, insisting on a clear-cut decision which calls for the winners to be right and the losers to admit that they were wrong.

• Using the fair argument in order to get your own way. "You went out last night, it's not fair for me to have to stay home." And then being upset because of the lack of fairness.

• Saying it isn't fair to the *kids,* my *parents,* or the *neighbors,* and consequently doing things that you'd rather not do and feeling resentment about it. Instead of blaming the entire mess on the lack of fairness, try looking hard at your own inability to decide for yourself what is most appropriate for you.

• The "If he can do it, so can I" game in which you justify something by someone else's behavior. This can be the neurotic rationale for cheating, stealing, flirting, lying, being late, or anything that you'd rather not admit into your own value system. On the highway, cutting off another driver because he did it to you, or hurrying up to get in front of a slowpoke, to slow him down, because he did it to you, or leaving your high-beams on because oncoming cars are doing it—literally putting your own life in jeopardy because your sense of justice has been violated. This is the "He hit me, so I hit him" routine that is largely employed by children who have seen this behavior thousands of times in their own parents. It is the cause of war when extended to its ridiculous extreme.

• Spending the same amount of money on a gift that someone else spent on one for you. Paying back every favor with a favor of equal value. Keeping the tally sheet equal, rather than doing what you would like in such matters. After all, "It has to be fair."

There they are, a brief excursion down Justice-Alley, where you, and those around you, find yourself internally shaken—often only slightly, but still shaken—because of that unserviceable sentence in your head that things must be fair.

Some of the Psychological Payoffs for Hanging on to Your "Demands for Justice"

The rewards for this kind of behavior are generally self-defeating in that they keep the focus off reality and on some kind of a dream world that will never exist. The most common reasons for retaining your "demand for justice" thinking and behavior are:

• You can feel smug with yourself for being honorable. It's one way to make yourself feel superior and better. As long as you insist on a mythological justice system for everything and are careful to keep your tally sheet in balance, you'll hold on to your holier than thou feeling and use up your present moments with smugness rather than effective living.

• You can give up responsibility for yourself and justify being immobilized by shifting the responsibility to those people and events that are not fair. A scape-goating for your lack of ability to be and feel what you choose. In this way, you can avoid risks, and the hard work of change. As long as injustice is the cause of your problems you can never change until the in-justice goes away, which, of course, it never will.

• Injustice can win you attention, pity and self-pity. The world has been unjust to you and now you and everyone around you must feel sorry for you. This is another great technique for avoiding change. The at-tention, pity and self-pity are your rewards, and you use them to prop yourself up rather than take charge of yourself and eliminate comparison behavior.

• You can justify all kinds of immoral, illegal and inappropriate behavior by making your action some-one else's responsibility. If he can do it, so can I. That's a beautiful rationalization system for any behavior.

• It gives you a sensational self-excuse for being ineffective. "If they aren't going to do anything, then neither am I." A clever little ploy for being too lazy, too tired, or too frightened.

• It gives you a conversation topic, and helps you to avoid talking about yourself to the people around you. Complain about all the injustices in the world and noth-ing gets done, but at least you killed those moments and maybe escaped dealing more honestly and per-sonally with each other.

• As long as you have a concept of justice, you can always make the just decision.

• You can manipulate others, particularly your chil-dren, by reminding them that they are being unfair to you if they aren't exactly the same as you, and don't keep a precise tally of all give-and-take in the rela-tionship. A nice little device for getting your own way.

• You can justify vindictive behavior because every-thing must be fair. This is a ploy for getting away with all kinds of manipulative and unsavory activities. Vengeance is justifiable because everything must be fair and even. Just as you must repay a favor, so you must repay a meanness.

There you have the psychological maintenance system for hanging on to demands for justice. But this support system is not unshakable. Below are some strategic methods for tossing out this kind of thinking and wiping clean this demand-for-justice erroneous zone.

Some Strategies for Giving Up the Futile Insistence on Justice

* Make a list of everything in your world that you think is unfair. Use your list as a guide for effective personal action. Ask yourself this important question: "Will the inequities go away if I am upset?" Obviously not. By attacking the erroneous thinking that brings about your upset, you will be on your way to escape from the justice trap.
* When you find yourself saying, "Would I do that to you?" or any similar sentence, change it to, "You are different from me, although I find that hard to accept right now." This will open, rather than close, communication between you and the other person.
* Begin to view your emotional life as independent of whatever anyone else does. This will free you from the chains of being hurt when others behave differently from the way you want them to.
* Try to view each decision not as a monumental life-changing event, but in perspective. Carlos Castaneda calls a man of knowledge one who—

Lives by acting, not by thinking about acting, nor by thinking about what he will think when he has finished acting . . . He knows that his life will be over altogether too soon; he knows, because he sees, that nothing is more important than anything else. . . . Thus a man of knowledge sweats and puffs and if one looks at him he is just like any ordinary man, except that the folly of his life is under control. Nothing being more important than anything else, a man of knowledge chooses any act, and acts it out as if it mattered to him. His controlled folly makes him say that what he does matters and makes him act as if it did, and yet he knows that it doesn't; so when he fulfills his acts he retreats in peace, and whether his acts were good or bad, or worked or didn't, is in no way any part of his concern.*

• Replace the sentence "It isn't fair" with "It's unfortunate," or "I'd prefer . . ." Thus, instead of insisting that the world be other than it is, you begin to accept reality—but not necessarily to approve of it.

• Eliminate external references of comparison. Have your own goals independent of what Tom, Dick or Harry do. Set out to be what you want, without references to what others have or don't have.

• Correct yourself out loud when you use a sentence such as, "I always call you when I'm going to be late, so why didn't you call me?" to "I would have felt better if you had called me." Thus you eliminate the erroneous notion that another's reason for calling is to become more like you.

• Rather than paying someone off, by bringing wine or a gift in exchange for dinner or a party, wait until you feel like it and then send a bottle of wine with a note saying, "Just because I think you're a great person." There's no need to balance the books with reciprocal trades; just do something nice because you, rather than a special occasion, call for it.

• Spend the amount of money you want to on any gift, and don't be swayed by what was spent for you. Eliminate invitations based on obligation and fairness.

* Carlos Castaneda, *A Separate Reality: Further Conversations with Don Juan* (New York: Pocket Books, 1972).

Decide whom you'll see on an internal rather than external standard.

• Set up your own standards of conduct in your family based upon what you think is appropriate for you. Have everyone else do the same. Then see if it isn't quite possible to make it happen without infringing on each other's rights. If you feel that being out three nights a week is what you want, but can't because someone has to watch the children, "fairness" doesn't have to enter into your decision-making. Perhaps you make some kind of baby-sitting arrangement, or have the kids go along, or whatever will be a mutually satisfying settlement. But to bring in the "It isn't fair" routine will surely lead to everyone's resentment—and to staying at home as well. Be a doer, not a complainer about injustice. For every injustice you suffer, there is a resolution that does not require you to be immobilized in any way.

• Remember that revenge is just another way of being controlled by others. Do what you, not they, decide is for you.

These are just a few beginning suggestions that will help you to be happier by ridding yourself of the need to compare yourself with others and to use their status as a barometer of your own happiness. It's not the injustice that counts, it's what you do about it.

IX
Putting an End to
Procrastination—Now

> It takes not one drop of sweat
> to put off doing anything.

Are you a procrastinator? If you're like most people, the answer to that is yes. But chances are that you'd rather not live with all that anxiety that accompanies putting things off as a way of life. You may find yourself postponing many tasks that you want to accomplish, and yet for some reason you just keep suspending action. This procrastination business is a mighty tiresome facet of life. If you've got a bad case, hardly a day goes by that you don't say, "I know I should be doing it, but I'll get around to it later." Your "putting it off" erroneous zone is difficult to blame on outside forces. It's all yours—both the putting off and the discomfort you endure as a result of it.

Procrastination is the closest there is to a universal erroneous zone. Very few people can honestly say that they are not procrastinators, despite the fact that it is unhealthy in the long run. As in all erroneous zones, there is nothing unhealthy about the behavior itself. Putting it off, in fact, doesn't even exist. You simply do, and those things you don't do, in reality, are just undone, rather than postponed. It is only the accompanying emotional reaction and immobilization that represent neurotic behavior. If you feel that you put things off, and like it, with no attending guilt, anxiety or upset, then by all means hang on to it, and pass over this chapter. However, for most people procrastination is really an escape from living present moments as fully as possible.

Hoping, Wishing and Maybe

Three neurotic phrases of the procrastinator make up the support system for maintaining putting-it-off behavior.

"I hope things will work out."
"I wish things were better."
"Maybe it'll be okay."

There you have the deferrer's delight. As long as you say maybe, or hope, or wish, you can use these as a rationale for not doing anything now. All wishing and hoping are a waste of time—the folly of fairyland residents. No amount of either ever got anything accomplished. They are merely convenient escape clauses from rolling up your sleeves and taking on the tasks that you've decided are important enough to be on your list of life activities.

You can do anything that you set your mind to accomplish. You are strong, capable and not the least bit brittle. But by putting things off for a future moment, you are giving in to escapism, self-doubt, and most significantly, self-delusion. Your putting it off zone is a movement away from being strong in your now, and toward the direction of hoping that things will improve in the future.

Inertia as a Strategy for Living

Here is a sentence that can keep you inert, in your present moments: "I'll wait, and it'll get better." For some this becomes a way of life—they are always putting it off for a day that can never arrive.

Mark, a recent client of mine, came to me complaining about his unhappy marriage. Mark was in his fifties and had been married for almost thirty years. As we began to talk about his marriage, it became clear that Mark's complaints were long-standing. "It's never been any good, even from the beginning," he said at one point. I asked Mark what had made him hold on for all these years of misery. "I kept hoping things would get better," he confessed. Almost thirty years of hope and Mark and his wife were still miserable.

As we talked more about Mark's life and marriage, he admitted to a history of impotence that went back at least a decade. Had he ever sought help for this problem, I asked. No, he had merely avoided sex more and more and hoped that the problem would go away on its own. "I was sure things would get better," Mark echoed his original comment.

Mark and his marriage were a classic case of inertia. He avoided his problems and justified his avoidance by saying, "If I wait and do nothing, maybe it'll work itself out." But Mark learned that things never work themselves out. They remain precisely as they are. At best, things change, but they don't get better. Things themselves (circumstances, situations, events, people) will not improve alone. If your life is better, it is because you have done something constructive to make it better.

Let's take a closer look at this procrastination behavior and how to eliminate it with some rather simple resolutions. This is one zone that you can clean up without a lot of hard "mental work," since it is one that you alone have created for yourself, without any of the cultural reinforcement that is the hallmark of so many other erroneous zones.

How Procrastination Works

Donald Marquis called procrastination "the art of keeping up with yesterday." To this I would add, "and avoiding today." This is how it works. You know there are certain things you want to do, not because others have so dictated, but because they are your deliberate choices. However, many of them never get done, despite your telling yourself that they will. Resolving to do something in the future which you could do now is an acceptable substitute for doing it, and permits you to delude yourself that you are really not compromising yourself by not doing what you have set out to do. It's a handy system that works something like this. "I know I must do that, but I'm really afraid that I might not do it well, or I won't like doing it. So, I'll tell myself that I'll do it in the future, then I don't have to admit to myself that I'm not going to do it. And it is easier to accept myself this way." This is the sort of convenient if fallacious reasoning that can be brought into play when you are faced with having to do something which is unpleasant or difficult.

If you are a person who lives one way and says you are going to live another way in the future, those proclamations are empty. You are simply a person who is always adjourning and never getting things done.

There are, of course, degrees of procrastination. It is possible to put things off up to a point, and then complete a task just prior to the deadline. Here again is a common form of self-delusion. If you allow yourself an absolute minimum amount of time to get your work done, then you can justify sloppy results or less than top-notch performance by saying to yourself, "I just didn't have enough time." But you have plenty of time. You know that busy people get things done. But if you spend your time complaining about how much you have to do (procrastination), then you'll have no present-moment time for doing it.

I once had a colleague who was a procrastination

specialist. He was always busy chasing down deals and talking about how much he had to do. When he talked, others got tired just imagining the pace of his life. But a close look would reveal that my colleague actually did very little. He had a zillion projects going in his mind and never got down to work on any of them. I imagine that each night before dozing off, he deluded himself with a promise that tomorrow he would get that job finished. How else could he go off to sleep with his self-delusional system intact? He may have known that he would not, but so long as he swore that he would, his present moments were safe.

You are not necessarily what you say. Behavior is a much better barometer of what you are than words. What you do in your present moments is the only indicator of what you are as a person. Emerson wrote,

Do not say things. What you are stands over you the while, and thunders so that I cannot hear what you say to the contrary.

Next time as you say you'll get it done, but know that you won't, keep those words in mind. They are the antidote to procrastination.

Critics and Doers

Putting it off as a way of life is one technique that you can use to avoid doing. A non-doer is very often a critic, that is, someone who sits back and watches doers, and then waxes philosophically about how the doers are doing. It is easy to be a critic, but being a doer requires effort, risk and change.

THE CRITIC

Our culture is full of critics. We even pay to hear them.

As you observe yourself and the people around you,

take note of how much social intercourse is devoted to criticism. Why? Because it is just plain easier to talk about how someone else has performed than to be the performer. Take note of real champions, those who have sustained a high level of excellence over a period of time. The Henry Aarons, the Johnny Carsons, the Bobby Fishers, the Katharine Hepburns, the Joe Louises, and people of that ilk. Doers at the highest levels. Champions in every way. Do they sit around poking serious criticism at others? The real doers of the world have no time for criticizing others. They're too busy doing. They work. They help others who are not as talented, rather than serve as their critics.

Constructive criticism can be useful. But if you've chosen the role of an observer rather than a doer, you are not growing. Moreover, you may be using your criticism to absolve yourself of the responsibility for your own ineffectiveness by projecting it onto those who are really making an effort. You can learn to ignore the fault-finders and self-appointed critics. Your first strategy will be to recognize these same behaviors in yourself, and resolve to eliminate them entirely, so that you can be a doer rather than a procrastinating critic.

Boredom: A Spin-Off of Procrastination

Life is never boring but some people choose to be bored. The concept of boredom entails an inability to use up present moments in a personally fulfilling way. Boredom is a choice; something you visit upon yourself, and it is another of those self-defeating items that you can eliminate from your life. When you procrastinate, you use your present moments doing nothing, as an alternative to doing anything. Doing nothing leads to boredom. The tendency is to blame boredom on the environment. "This town is really dull" or "What a boring speaker." The particular town or speaker is never dull, it is you experiencing the boredom, and you can eliminate it by doing something else with your mind or energy at that moment.

Samuel Butler said, "The man who lets himself be bored is even more contemptible than the bore." By doing what you choose, now, or using your mind in creative new ways now, you can insure that you'll never again choose boredom for yourself. The choice, as always, is yours.

Some Typical Procrastinating Behavior

Here are some areas where procrastination is a much easier choice than action.

• Staying in a job in which you find yourself stuck and unable to grow.

• Hanging onto a relationship that has gone sour. Staying married (or unmarried) and merely hoping that it will get better.

• Refusing to work on relationship difficulties such as sex, shyness or phobias. Simply waiting for them to improve, instead of trying to do something constructive about them.

• Not tackling addictions such as alcoholism, drugs, pills, or smoking. Saying, "I'll quit when I'm ready," but knowing that you are putting it off because you doubt that you can.

• Putting off arduous or menial tasks such as cleaning, repairing, sewing, lawn work, painting and the like —providing you really care about whether or not they get done. If you wait long enough, maybe it will get done by itself.

• Avoiding a confrontation with others, such as an authority figure, a friend, a lover, a salesperson or a serviceman. By waiting, you end up not having to do it, although the confrontation might have improved the relationship or the service.

• Being afraid to change locations geographically. You stay in the same place for a lifetime.

• Putting off spending a day or an hour with your children which you might enjoy because you have too much work or are bogged down in serious matters. Similarly, not going out for an evening to dinner, or to the theater or a sports event with your loved ones and using your "I'm busy" line to postpone it forever.

• Deciding to start your diet tomorrow or next week. It's easier to put-it-off than to take-it-off, so you say, "I'll get to it tomorrow," which of course will never arrive.

• Using sleep or tiredness as a reason for putting it off. Did you ever notice how tired you get when you are close to actually doing something uncomfortable or difficult? A little fatigue is a terrific deferring device.

• Getting sick when you are faced with a disquieting or troublesome task. How could you possibly do it now, when you feel so terrible? Like exhaustion above, it's an excellent technique for procrastinating.

• The "I don't have time to do it" ruse, in which you justify not doing something because of your busy schedule, which always has room for those things that you really want to do.

• Constantly looking forward to a vacation or that dream-trip. Next year we'll find Nirvana.

• Being a critic and using your criticism of others to camouflage your own refusal to do.

• Refusing to get a physical checkup when you suspect some dysfunction. By putting it off you don't have to deal with the reality of possible illness.

• Being afraid to make a move toward someone you're fond of. It's what you want, but you'd rather wait it out and hope that things work out.

• Being bored at any time in your life. This is merely a way of putting off something and using the boring event as a reason for not doing something more exciting.

• Planning but never putting in action a regular exercise program. "I'll get started on that right away . . . next week."

• Living your entire life for your children and always putting off your own happiness. How can we afford a vacation when we have the kids' education to worry about?

Reasons for Continuing to Put It Off

The rationale for putting it off is composed of one part self-delusion and two parts escape. Here are the most important rewards for hanging on to procrastination.

• Most obviously, putting it off allows you to escape from unpleasant activities. There may be things you're afraid to do or things part of you wants to do and part of you doesn't. Remember, nothing is black or white.
• You can feel comfortable with your self-delusional system. Lying to yourself keeps you from having to admit that you are not a "doer" in this particular present moment.
• You can stay exactly as you are forever, as long as you keep putting it off. Thus you eliminate change and all the risks that go with it.
• By being bored you have someone or something else to blame for your unhappy state, thus you shift responsibility away from yourself and onto the boring activity.
• By being a critic you can feel important at the expense of others. It is a way of using others' performance as stepping-stones for elevating yourself in your own mind. More self-delusion.
• By waiting for things to get better you can blame the world for your unhappiness—things just never seem to break for you. A great strategy for doing nothing.
• You can avoid ever having to fail by avoiding all activities which involve some risk. In this way you never have to come face to face with your self-doubt.
• Wishing for things to happen—Santa Claus fantasies—allows you to return to a safe and protected childhood.
• You can win sympathy from others and feel sorry

for yourself for the anxiety that you live with as a result of not doing what you'd like to have done.

• You are able to justify a sloppy or less than acceptable performance on anything if you put it off long enough, and then just allow a minimal time segment for getting it done. "But I just didn't have time."

• By putting it off, you might be able to get someone else to do it for you. Thus, procrastination becomes a means of manipulating others.

• Putting it off enables you to delude yourself into believing that you are something other than what you really are.

• By avoiding a task you can escape success. If you don't succeed you avoid having to feel good about yourself and accepting all of the continuing responsibility that goes with success.

Now that you have some insight into why you procrastinate, you can begin to do something about eliminating this self-destructive erroneous zone.

Some Techniques for Ousting This Postponing Behavior

• Make a decision to live five minutes at a time. Instead of thinking of tasks in long-range terms, think about now and try to use up a five-minute period doing what you want, refusing to put off anything that would bring about satisfaction.

• Sit down and get started on something you've been postponing. Begin a letter or a book. You'll find that much of your putting it off is unnecessary since you'll very likely find the job enjoyable, once you give up the procrastination. Simply beginning will help you to eliminate anxiety about the whole project.

• Ask yourself, "What is the worst thing that could happen to me if I did what I'm putting off right now?" The answer is usually so insignificant that it may jar you into action. Assess your fear and you'll have no reason to hang on to it.

• Give yourself a designated time slot (say Wednesday from 10:00 to 10:15 P.M.) which you will devote exclusively to the task you've been putting off. You'll discover that the fifteen minutes of devoted effort are often sufficient to see you over the hump of procrastination.

• Think of yourself as too significant to live with anxiety about the things you have to do. So, the next time you know you are uncomfortable with postponement anxiety, remember that people who love themselves don't hurt themselves that way.

• Look carefully at your now. Decide what you are avoiding in your current moments and begin to tackle the fear of living effectively. Procrastination is substituting the now with anxiety about a future event. If the event becomes the now, the anxiety, by definition, must go.

• Quit smoking . . . now! Begin your diet . . . this moment! Give up booze . . . this second. Put this book down and do one push-up as your beginning exercise project. That's how you tackle problems . . . with action now! Do it! The only thing holding you back is you, and the neurotic choices you've made because you don't believe you're as strong as you really are. How simple . . . just do it!

• Start using your mind creatively in what were previously boring circumstances. At a meeting, change the dull tempo with a pertinent question, or make your mind go off in exciting ways such as writing a poem, or memorizing twenty-five numbers backwards, just for the sheer drill of memory training. Decide to never be bored again.

• When someone begins to criticize you, ask this question, "Do you think I need a critic now?" Or when you find yourself being a critic, ask the person in your company if he wants to hear your criticism, and if so, why? This will help you to move from the critic to the doer column.

• Look hard at your life. Are you doing what you'd choose to be doing if you knew you had six months to live? If not, you'd better begin doing it because, relatively speaking, that's all you have. Given the eternity of time, thirty years or six months make no difference. Your total lifetime is a mere speck. Delaying anything makes no sense.

• Be courageous about undertaking an activity that you've been avoiding. One act of courage can eliminate all that fear. Stop telling yourself that you must perform well. Remind yourself that doing it is far more important.

• Decide not to be tired until the moment before you get into bed. Don't allow yourself to use fatigue or illness as an escape or to put off doing anything. You may find that when you take away the reason for the illness or exhaustion—that is, avoidance of a task—physical problems "magically" disappear.

• Eliminate the words "hope," "wish" and "maybe" from your vocabulary. They are the tools of putting it off. If you see these words creeping in, substitute new sentences. Change

"I hope things will work out" to "I will make it happen."

"I wish things were better" to "I am going to do the following things to ensure that I feel better."

"Maybe it will be okay" to "I will make it okay."

• Keep a journal of your own complaining or critical behavior. By writing these actions down, you'll accomplish two things. You'll see how your critical behavior surfaces in your life—the frequency, patterns, events and people that are related to your being a critic. You'll also stop yourself from criticizing because it will be such a pain to have to write in the journal.

• If you are putting something off which involves others (a move, a sex problem, a new job), have a conference with all involved and ask their opinions. Be courageous about talking of your own fears, and see if you are delaying for reasons that are only in your head. By enlisting the aid of a confidant to help you with your procrastination, you'll have made it a joint effort. Soon you'll dissipate much of the anxiousness that goes along with procrastination by sharing that as well.

• Write a contract with your loved ones in which you will deliver the goods you want to but which you may have been postponing. Have each party keep a copy of the contract, and build in penalties for defaulting. Whether it's a ball game, dinner out, vacation, or theater visit, you'll find this strategy helpful and personally rewarding, since you'll be participating in events that you also find enjoyable.

If you want the world to change, don't complain about it. Do something. Rather than using up your present moments with all kinds of immobilizing anxiety over what you are putting off, take charge of this nasty erroneous zone and live now! Be a doer, not a wisher, hoper or critic.

X
Declare Your
Independence

In any relationship in which two people become one, the end result is two half people.

Leaving the psychological nest is one of life's difficult chores. The dependency viper intrudes in life in many, many ways, and routing it entirely is made more difficult by the numerous people who benefit from another's psychological dependency. Psychological independence means total freedom from all obligatory relationships, and an absence of other-directed behavior. It means being free from having to do something you would not otherwise choose, were the relationship not to exist. The nest-leaving business is especially difficult because our society teaches us to fulfill certain expectations in special relationships, which include parents, children, authority figures and loved ones.

Leaving the nest means becoming your own person, living and choosing the behaviors that you want. It does not mean breaking off in any sense of the word. If you enjoy your way of interacting with anyone and it doesn't interfere with your own goals, then it is something you can cherish rather than change. Psychological dependence, on the other hand, means that you are in relationships that involve no choice, a relationship in which you are obliged to be something you don't want to be and that you resent the way in which you are being forced to conduct yourself. This is the guts of this erroneous zone, and it is akin to the approval-seeking discussed in Chapter III. If you want some kind of relationship, then it is not unhealthy. But if you need it, or are forced into it, and subsequently feel resentment, then you are in a self-defeating area. Thus, it is the obligation that is the problem, rather than the relationship itself. Obligation breeds guilt and dependency, while choice fosters love and independence. There is no choice in a psychologically dependent relationship, consequently there will always be indignation and ill-feelings in any such alliance.

Being psychologically independent involves not needing others. I didn't say wanting others, I said needing. The moment you need, you become vulnerable, a slave. If the one you need leaves, or changes his mind, or dies, you are then forced into immobilization, collapse, or even death. But society teaches us to be psychologically dependent on a whole raft of folks from parents on, and you still may be holding open your mouth waiting for the worms in many significant relationships. As long as you feel that you have to do anything because it is expected of you in a particular relationship, and your doing it creates any resentment or your not doing it any guilt, you can count yourself as having work to do in this erroneous zone.

Eliminating dependency starts with your family, with the way your parents dealt with you as a child and the way you deal with your own children today. How many psychologically dependent sentences do you carry in your head today? How many of them do you force on your children?

The Dependency Trap in Child Rearing and the Family

Walt Disney produced a superb film some years ago entitled *Bear Country*. It traced a mother bear and her two babies through the first few months of the cubs' lives. Mama-bear taught the cubs how to hunt, fish and climb trees. She taught them how to protect themselves when they confronted danger. Then one day, Mama-bear, for her own instinctive reasons, decided that it was time to leave. She forced them to scamper up a tree, and without even looking back, she left. Forever! In her own bear mind, she had completed her parental responsibilities. She didn't try to manipulate them into visiting her on alternate Sundays. She did not accuse them of being ungrateful, or threaten to have a nervous breakdown if they disappointed her. She simply let them go. Throughout the animal kingdom, parenting means to teach the offspring the skills necessary to be independent and then to leave. With us humans, the instinct is still the same, that is, to be independent, but the neurotic need to own and live one's life through one's children seems to take over, and the goal of raising a child to be independent is subverted into the idea of raising a child to hold onto him.

What do you want for your children? Would you like them to be high in self-esteem and self-confidence, neurosis-free, fulfilled and happy? Of course you would. But how can you help to ensure such an outcome? Only by being that way yourself. Children learn from the behavior of their models. If you are full of guilt and unfulfilled in your life, but telling your children not to be, then you are selling a tainted product. If you model low self-esteem, then you'll teach your children to adopt the same attitudes for themselves. Even more significantly, if you make your children more important than yourself, you are not helping them, you are merely teaching them to put others ahead of themselves, and to take a back seat while remaining unfulfilled. Such irony. You cannot hand your children self-confidence; they must acquire it by seeing you living the same way yourself. Only by treating yourself as the most important person and not always sacrificing yourself for your children will you teach them to have their own self-confidence and belief in themselves. If you are a sacrificer, you are modeling sacrificing behavior. And what does sacrificing behavior mean? Putting others before yourself, not liking yourself, seeking approval and other erroneous behavior. While doing for others is sometimes admirable, if it is at the expense of yourself, you are merely teaching the others the same kind of resentment-breeding behavior.

From the very beginning children want to do things for themselves. "I can do it myself!" "Watch me, Mommy, I can do it without any help." "I'll feed myself." On and on the signals come. And while there is a great deal of dependence in those early years, there is also the distinctive push toward autonomy almost from the first day.

As a four-year-old, little Roxanne will always come to Mommy and Daddy when she is hurt or in need of an emotional support of any sort. She pours out her soul when she is eight and ten years of age. While she wants to be thought of as a big girl ("I'll button my own coat!"), she also wants the support of a caring parent. ("Look Mom, I scratched my knee and it's bleeding.") Her self-concept is developing through the views of her parents and other significant people in her life. Suddenly, Roxanne is fourteen. She comes home crying because of a fight with her boyfriend, and she runs into her bedroom, slamming the door behind her. Mama comes up and asks her to talk about it in her typically caring way. But now she is told by Roxanne in no uncertain terms, "I don't want to talk about it. Leave me alone." Instead of Mama understanding that this little scene is evidence that she has been an effective parent, and the little Roxanne who always told all her problems to Mommy is now working on them herself (emotional independence), Mama is distressed. She is not ready to let go, to let Roxanne work it out in her own independent way. She still sees Roxanne as the same nestling that she was only a short time ago. But if Mama persists, and forces the issue, she will be in for a huge dose of resentment from Roxanne.

The child's desire to get out of the nest is strong, but when ownership and sacrifice have been the lubrication for the family machine, the natural act of leaving turns into a crisis. Nest-leaving in a psychologically sound atmosphere involves neither crisis nor turmoil; it is the natural consequence of effective living. But when guilt and fear of disappointment color the nest-leaving, they continue throughout life, sometimes to the point that the marriage relationship becomes one of parenting, rather than of two individuals sharing on an equal footing.

What then are your goals of parenting, and of working out an effective present relationship with your own parents? Certainly the family is an important unit in the developmental process, but it should not be a permanent unit. It should not be a vehicle of guilt and neurosis when its various members make moves for emotional independence. You may have heard parents say, "I have a right to make my child into anything I choose." But what is the payoff for such a domineering attitude? Hate, resentment, anger and frustrating guilt when the child grows up. As you examine effective parent-child relationships which have no requirements or obligations attached, you'll discover parents who treat their children as friends. If a child spills the catsup on the table, it's not a "Why don't you watch what you're doing; you're so clumsy" routine. Instead, you'll see the same kind of a response that would be given to a friend were they to spill something. "Can I help you?" No abuse because they are owned, but a respect for the child's dignity. You'll also discover that effective parents foster independence rather than dependence, and create no scenes about normal desires to be autonomous.

Differences Between Dependent and Independent Focused Families

In families that focus on independence, movement toward being one's own person is seen as normal, rather than as a challenge to anyone's authority. Clinging and needing are not emphasized. Similarly, there are no demands that a child have allegiance forever, simply because of membership in a family. The result is family members who want to be together, rather than feel obligated to be together. There is also a respect for privacy rather than a demand to share everything. In families like this, the woman has a life of her own beyond being a mother and wife. She will model effective living for her children, rather than live her life for and through them. The parents feel that their own happiness is paramount, because without it there can be no family harmony. Hence the parents can go off alone occasionally, and not feel obliged to always be there for their children. The mother isn't a slave, because she doesn't want her own children (especially the girls) to become one. And she doesn't want to be one herself. She doesn't feel that she must be there all the time for her infant's every need. She feels that she can appreciate her children and vice versa all the more if she is fulfilling herself and contributing to her family, her community and her culture on an equal footing with the men in this world.

In this sort of family there is no subtle manipulation via guilt or threats to keep the children dependent and responsible to the parents. As the children mature, the parents don't want their kids to visit them out of obligation. Besides, the parents are too busy being effective in their own way to be sitting around waiting for children and grandchildren to show up and give them a reason for living. Parents like these don't believe that they should spare their own children all of the hardships that they suffered because they recognize that the very act of working at a hardship is what gave them their own self-confidence and self-esteem. They wouldn't want to rob their children of such precious experiences.

These parents perceive the desire of their children to struggle for themselves, with the assistance but not overbearance of a caring parent, as healthy and not to be denied. Hesse's Demian talks about the variety of paths to independence.

Sooner or later each of us must take the step that separates him from his father, from his mentors;

each of us must have some cruelly lonely experience . . . I myself had not parted from my parents and their world, the "luminous" world in a violent struggle, but had gradually and almost imperceptibly become estranged. I was sad that it had to be this way, and it made for many unpleasant hours during my visits back home.*

You can have all visits back home be fond experiences, if you get a firm handle on your own struggle for independence from your parents. And if you model self-pride and self-worth for your children, they will in turn leave the nest with an absence of stress and turmoil for all concerned.

Dorothy Canfield Fisher summed it up perfectly in *Her Son's Wife:*

A mother is not a person to lean on, but a person to make leaning unnecessary.

So be it. You can make nest-leaving a natural event, or one which is loaded with trauma and which will haunt the child and the relationship forever. But you were also a child at one time, and if you learned the psychological dependency routine well, then perhaps when you married you substituted one dependent relationship for another.

Psychological Dependence and Marriage Crisis

You may have resolved your dependency on your parents, and perhaps your relationship with your own children is under control as well. Perhaps you recognize your children's need for independence and are encouraging it. But you may still have a dependency problem in your life. If you're one of those people who left one dependent relationship with your parents and en-

---

* Hermann Hesse, *Demian* (New York: Bantam Books, 1974), p. 104.

tered into another when you married, then you have an erroneous zone that needs work.

Louis Anspacher wrote about marriage in America—

Marriage is that relation between man and woman in which the independence is equal, the dependence mutual, and the obligation reciprocal.

There they are, the two ugly words, dependence and obligation, which account for the state of marriage and rate of divorce in our country. The simple fact is that most folks just don't like marriage, and while they may endure it, or get out of it, the psychological casualties persist.

A relationship based on love, as was said earlier, is one in which each partner allows the other to be what he chooses, with no expectations and no demands. It is a simple association of two people who love each other so much that each would never expect the other to be something that he wouldn't choose for himself. It is a union based on independence, rather than dependence. But this sort of relationship is so rare in our culture that it is almost mythological. Imagine a union with the one you love, in which each of you can be whatever you desire. Now consider the reality of most relationships. How does that grisly dependency sneak in and muck up the works?

A Typical Marriage

The thread that winds through most marriages is one of dominance and submission. While the roles may shift regularly, different for various marital situations, the thread is nevertheless present. One partner dominates the other as a condition of the alliance. A case history of a typical marriage and its psychological crisis points goes something like that of our fictional couple below.

At the time of marriage, the husband is twenty-three

and his wife is twenty. He has slightly more education, and has secured the money-earning prestige position, while the woman works as a secretary, clerk, or perhaps in a profession dominated by women such as teacher or nurse. The woman's job is a filler, until she can become a mother. After four years of marriage, there are two or three children, and the woman is serving as a wife and mother in the home. Her role is that of taking care of the house, her children and her husband. From a job standpoint, her position is that of a domestic, and psychologically she is in a submissive position. The man's work is given more significance, largely because he brings in money to support the family. His successes become his wife's successes, and his social contacts become their friends. He is given more status in the home, and the woman's role is often one of making his life as comfortable as she can. The woman spends the greater part of her day interacting with children or she talks with neighborhood women who are in the same psychological snare. When her husband has a crisis on the job, it becomes her crisis, and generally speaking, any objective observer would see that there is a dominant and a submissive member in this arrangement. The woman has accepted and perhaps sought out this kind of relationship, because it is all she has ever known. Her marriage is modeled on that of her parents and others she saw as she grew up. And more often than not, her dependence on her husband merely replaced her dependence on her parents. The man similarly sought out a woman who was soft spoken, gentle, and who would reinforce the fact that he was the breadwinner and headwinner in all interactions. Thus, both people got what they were looking for, and what they had seen all of their own lives in terms of how a marriage operates.

After several years of marriage, perhaps four to seven years, a crisis begins to erupt. The submissive partner begins to feel trapped, unimportant and dissatisfied because she is not making a significant contribution. The man encourages his wife to be more her own person, to be more assertive, and to take charge of her life and stop feeling sorry for herself. These are the first messages that conflict with what he wanted when he got married. "If you want to work, why don't you look for a job?" or "Go back to school." He encourages her to seek new outlets, to stop being so namby-pamby. In short, to be something different than what he married, which was submissive and domestic. The woman, until now, has always felt that any unhappiness in her husband was her fault. "Where did I go wrong?" If he's unhappy or frustrated, she feels that she has been inadequate, or that she must not be as attractive as she used to be. The submissive partner resorts to her own subservient mind-set, and assesses all male problems as being lodged in her own self.

At this time in the marriage the man is very much occupied with job promotions, social contacts and professional striving. He is on his way up, and a sniveling wife is something he cannot tolerate. Because of his many opportunities to deal with a great number of different people (something denied to his submissive partner) he is changing. He has become even more self-assertive, demanding and intolerant of weaknesses in others, including his family. Thus, his admonitions to "get yourself together" to his submissive wife. This is also a time when the husband may look for sexual outlets outside the marriage. He has many opportunities and he seeks the companionship of more exciting women. Sometimes the submissive partner begins some experimentation of her own. She may take on a volunteer job, enroll in school, seek therapy, have an affair of her own, *most* of which is enthusiastically supported by the husband.

Perhaps the submissive partner will begin to gain new insights into her behavior. She sees her subservience as something that she has chosen all her life, not just in her marriage. Her approval-seeking behavior has now been challenged, and she begins to put herself on the road to greater self-responsibility by eliminating all dependency in her world, including that of her parents, her husband, her friends, and even her children. She begins to gain self-confidence. She may take on a job, and begin to make new friends. She begins to stand up to her dominant husband, and stops taking all of the abuse that has been her lot since the marriage began. She demands equality, no longer satisfied to wait any longer for it to be granted to her. She simply takes it. She insists on a sharing of domestic chores, including care of the children.

This new independence and the shift from the external to internal thinking on the part of the woman is not easily accepted by her husband. He becomes threatened. Anxiety is entering his life at a time when he cannot afford it. The last thing he needs is an upstart wife, even though he encouraged her to get out more on her own and think for herself. He didn't expect to create a monster, least of all one that would challenge his own established supremacy. He may react with a heavy dose of dominance, which has always worked at putting his submissive partner in her place in the past. He argues against the absurdity of working, when she is paying most all of her salary for baby-sitters. He points to the illogic of her belief that she isn't equal. In fact, she's indulged. "You don't have to work, you have it made, all you have to do is take care of a house and be a mother to your children." He tries guilt. "The children are going to suffer." "I can't have this aggravation." Perhaps he threatens her with divorce, or as a last resort, suicide. This often works. The wife says to herself, "Wow, I almost blew it," and reverts to her submissive role. The heavy dose of dominance served to remind her of her place. But if she refuses to regress, the marriage itself may be in jeopardy. At any rate, there is a definite crisis. If the wife persists in replacing her submissiveness with self-reliance, the husband, who needs to dominate someone, might leave for a younger wife who will stand in awe of him and thus put her in the position of looking up to him and becoming a cute little showpiece. On the other hand, the marriage may survive the crisis, and an interesting shift may take place. The thread of dominance and submission still winds its way through the marriage. That is the only kind of marriage both partners recognize. Often the husband will now take on the submissive role out of fear of losing something he cherishes, or at least depends on. Staying home more, getting closer to the children (out of guilt from earlier abandonment), he may say things like, "You don't need me any more" or "You're changing, you're not the girl I married and I'm not sure I like the new you." He has become more submissive. He may become a heavy drinker, and a self-pitier out of a need to manipulate his wife or to recapture his long-lost superiority. The wife is now in a career, or moving toward one; she has her own circle of friends, and is developing outside interests of her own. Perhaps she is having an affair as an assertive retaliatory gesture, but at the least, she is feeling good about receiving some acclaim and compliments for her accomplishments. However, the thread is still there, and a crisis looms heavy. As long as one partner must be more important than the other or fear-of-divorce is the thing that binds the two together, dependency is still the cornerstone of the alliance. The dominant partner, be it man or woman, is not satisfied with a slave for a spouse. The marriage may continue in a legal sense, but any love or communication between the two partners has been destroyed. Divorce is common here, but if not, two people begin to go their separate ways within the marriage—no sex, separate quarters, a communication pattern based on mutual put-down, in lieu of understanding.

A different conclusion is also possible, if both partners decide to reevaluate themselves and their relationship. If both work at becoming free of erroneous zones, and loving each other in the sense of allowing the other partner to choose his own fulfillment, then the marriage can flower and grow. With two self-reliant people, who care enough about each other to foster independence rather than dependence, but at the same time share happiness with a loved person, marriage can be an exciting prospect. But, when two people try to merge into one-ness, or one tries to dominate the other in any way, that spark that is within us all fights for one of the greatest human needs, independence.

Longevity is not an indication of success in marriage. Many people stay married out of fear of the unknown, or because of inertia, or simply because it is the thing to do. In a successful marriage, a marriage where both partners feel genuine love, each is willing to let the other person choose for himself rather than to dominate. There is not the constant hassling that involves thinking and speaking for the other partner, and demanding that he does what he's supposed to. Dependency is the ser-pent in the paradise of a happy marriage. It creates patterns of dominance and submission and ultimately destroys relationships. This erroneous zone can be elim-inated, but it will never be an easy battle, since power and control are at stake, and few want to give them up without a fight. Most important, dependency should not be confused with love. Putting some spaces in to-getherness ironically solidifies marriages.

You Are Treated the Way You Teach Others to Treat You

Dependency is not something that just happens be-cause of association with domineering people. It is, like all erroneous zone behavior, a choice. You teach peo-ple to dominate you, and to treat you the way you've always been treated. There are many schemes that maintain the domineering process, and they are re-peated only if they work. They work if they keep you in line and in a dependent position in the relationship. Here are some of the common strategies for maintain-ing dominance and control threads in marriage.

• Yelling, screaming and voice-raising of any kind. This will keep you in line if you are a soft person and want things quiet and smooth.

- Threatening behavior such as, "I'll leave, I'll get a divorce."
- Inducement of guilt. "You had no right to——" "I don't understand how you could have done such a thing." If guilt is your hang-up, then you can be kept "submissive" with such statements.
- The use of anger and explosive behavior, such as throwing things, swearing, hitting objects.
- The physical ailment ploy. Having a heart attack, headache, back problem, or whatever when one partner doesn't act the way the other wants him to. You can be manipulated by this if you have taught your partner that you'll behave when he gets sick.
- The silent treatment. No talking and deliberate sulking are superlative strategies that one partner can use to maneuver the other into correct behavior
- The tears routine in which you cry in order to help the other person to feel guilty.
- The leaving scene. Simply getting up and walking out is a good way to manipulate a partner into or out of certain behavior.
- The "You don't love me" or "You don't understand me" contrivance for getting one's way and maintaining the dependency in the relationship.
- The suicide scheme. "If you don't do what I want, then I'll kill myself" or "If you leave me, I'll end it all."

All of the above strategies are methods that keep the other person in the desired role in marriage. They are used when they work. If one partner refuses to be manipulated by them, the other will not continue to use them. It is only when one mate is responsive to these ploys that the other gets in the habit of using them. If you give the proper submissive reactions, you are teaching the other what you will tolerate.

If you get pushed around, you've been sending push-me-around signals. You can learn to teach others to treat you the way you want to be treated. It will take time and effort because it has taken a lot of time to teach others how you wanted to be treated until now.

But you can make the change whether it be on the job, in the family, at a restaurant, on the bus, any place at all that you receive shabby treatment which you dislike. Rather than saying, "Why don't you treat me better?" begin to say, "What am I doing to teach others to treat me this way?" Put the focus on you, and begin changing those reactions.

Some Common Dependency and Dependency-Fostering Behavior

* Feeling unable to leave the nest or leaving it with bad feelings on both sides.
* Feeling required or obliged to visit, telephone, entertain, chauffeur and the like.
* Asking permission of a spouse for anything, including spending money, authority to speak, or use of the car.
* Invasion of privacy, such as looking through drawers and private records of children.
* Sentences like, "I could never tell him how I feel, he wouldn't like it."
* Falling into depression and immobilization after the death of a loved one.
* Feeling committed to a particular job and never venturing out on your own.
* Having expectations for how a spouse, parent, or child has to be.
* Being embarrassed by a child's, spouse's, or parent's behavior, as if what they are is a part of what you are.
* Being in *training* all of your life for a job or position. Never leaving the training phase for self-reliance.
* Being hurt by what others say, feel, think, or do.
* Only feeling happy or successful if your mate is feeling that way.
* Taking orders from someone.
* Allowing someone else to make decisions for you, or always asking advice before deciding.

• "You owe me, look what I did for you." The obligations that go with being dependent.

• Not doing something in front of a parent or dominant person because they wouldn't approve. Not smoking, drinking, swearing, eating a hot fudge sundae, or whatever, because of your submissive role.

• Giving up on your own life when a loved one dies, or becomes seriously ill.

• Using careful language around a dominant person, so that he won't be upset with you.

• Persistently lying about your own behavior, and having to distort the truth so that "they" won't be upset with you.

The Psychological Compensation of Dependency

The reasons for hanging on to this self-thwarting behavior are not very complicated. You may know the payoffs for being a dependent, but do you know how destructive they are? Dependency may appear harmless, but it is the enemy of all happiness and fulfillment. Here are the more common dividends for keeping yourself in a dependent state:

• Being dependent can keep you in the protective custody of others, and give you the little child benefits of not being responsible for your own behavior.

• By staying dependent, you can blame your shortcomings on others.

• If you are dependent on others, you don't have to undertake the hard work and risk of change. You are secure in your reliance on others who will take responsibility for you.

• You can feel good about yourself because you are pleasing others. You learned that the way to be good is to please Mommy, and now many symbolic Mommies manipulate you.

• You can avoid guilt which you choose when you

behave assertively. It is easier to behave than to learn to eliminate guilt.

• You needn't make choices or decisions for yourself. You model yourself on the parent, spouse, or individual on whom you depend. So long as you think what they think or feel what they feel, there's no need for the hard work of determining what you think or feel.

• When everything else is boiled away, it is just plain easier to be a follower than a leader. You can do what you're told and avoid trouble, even though you may not like the way you feel as a follower. It's still simpler than taking all those risks that go with being your own person. Dependency is distasteful because it makes you into less than a whole, independently functioning person. But it is easier, that's for sure.

A Prospectus for Ridding Yourself of Dependency

• Write your own Declaration of Independence in which you spell out for yourself how you want to function in all relationships, not eliminating compromise, but wiping out any manipulation without representation. "I, the person, in order to have a more perfect union, etc."

• Talk with each person that you feel you are psychologically dependent upon. Declare your aims of functioning independently, explain how you feel when you do things out of a sense of obligation. This is an excellent strategy for getting started, because the other may not even be aware of how you feel as a dependent.

• Give yourself five-minute goals for how you're going to deal with dominant people in your life. Try a one-shot "No, I don't want to," and test the reaction of your reaction in the other person's.

• Arrange a planning session with your dominant partner at a time when you are feeling unthreatened. During this session, explain that you sometimes feel manipulated and submissive and that you would like to arrange a nonverbal signal to let the other person know how you are feeling when it crops up, but that you don't want to discuss it at that time. A simple tugging of the ear or a thumb in the mouth to signal you're feeling submissive at a particular time.

• At the moment you are feeling shoved-around psychologically, state how you feel to the person, and then act out the way you'd like to behave.

• Remind yourself that parents, spouses, friends, bosses, children and others will often disapprove of your behavior, and that has nothing to do with who or what you are. It is a given fact in any relationship that you will incur some disapproval. If you expect it, then you won't be thrown by it. In this way you can break many of the dependency ties that enslave you emotionally.

• Even if you are deliberately avoiding dominant people (parent, spouse, boss, child), you are still being controlled by them in their absence if you are experiencing emotional immobilization because of them.

• If you are feeling obligated to visit certain people, ask yourself if you would want others to visit you simply because they felt required to do so. If not, extend a similar courtesy to those you are treating in this manner, and talk it out with them. That is, reverse the logic and see how undignified a relationship of obligation really is.

• Make a decision to get out of your dependency role by doing volunteer work, reading, getting a baby-sitter (even if you can't afford it), getting a job that doesn't necessarily even pay well. Why? Simply because the remuneration of your own high self-esteem is worth whatever the price it costs in money or time.

• Insist on financial independence with no strings, and no accounting to anyone. You are a slave if you must ask for money. If that is impossible, arrange to make your own money in any creative way that you can devise.

• Let them go! Let yourself go! Stop giving orders! Stop taking orders!

• Recognize your desire for privacy and not having

to share everything you feel and experience with someone. You are unique and private. If you feel you must share everything then you are without choice, and of course, a dependent.

• Let a child's room be his. Give him an area that he can control, and, as long as it's not unhealthy, allow him to make decisions about how it will be organized. A made bed is not any more psychologically sound than an unmade bed, even though you may have learned the opposite.

• At a party, congregate with people away from your partner. Don't feel responsible to be with that person at all times. Split up and then join forces when it is over. You'll double your learning and experience.

• If you want to go to a movie and your partner wants to play tennis, do it that way! Allow yourself more separateness, and your moments of togetherness will be happier, and more exciting.

• Take mini-trips alone, or with friends without having to feel attached to your partner. You'll feel more strongly toward your partner when you come back, and you'll treasure your independent functioning as well.

• Keep in mind that you have no responsibility to make others happy. Others make themselves happy. Thus, you may truly enjoy the company of another, but if you feel it is your mission to make them happy, then you are a dependent who will also feel gloom when the other person is down. Or even worse, you'll feel as though you let him down. You are responsible for your own emotions and so is everyone else. No one has control over your feelings, except you.

• Remember that habit is no reason to do anything. Just because you've always been submissive to others is not sufficient justification for allowing it to continue.

The business of effective living and parenting is independence. Similarly, the hallmark of effective marriage is minimal fusion and optimal autonomy and self-reliance. And while you may feel real fear about breaking away from dependent relationships, if you asked those upon whom you are emotionally dependent, you would surprisingly discover that they most admire those who think and act for themselves. More irony. You get the most respect for being independent, particularly from those who try the hardest to keep you subordinate.

The nest is a beautiful place for a child to develop, but nest-leaving is even more beautiful and can be viewed that way by the one leaving, as well as the one watching the takeoff.

XI
Farewell to Anger

The only antidote to anger is to eliminate the internal sentence, "If only you were more like me."

Is your fuse too short? You may accept anger as a part of your life, but do you recognize that it serves no utilitarian purpose? Perhaps you've justified your short-fuse behavior by saying things like, "It's only human," or "If I don't express it, then I'll store it up and have an ulcer." But anger is probably a part of you that you don't like, and needless to say, neither does anyone else.

Anger is not "only human." You do not have to possess it, and it serves no purpose that has anything to do with being a happy, fulfilled person. It is an erroneous zone, a kind of psychological influenza that incapacitates you just as a physical disease would.

Let's define the term *anger*. As used in this chapter, it refers to an immobilizing reaction, experienced when any expectancy is not met. It takes the form of rage, hostility, striking out at someone or even glowering silence. It is not simple annoyance or irritation. Once again the key word is immobility. Anger is immobilizing and it is usually a result of wishing the world and the people in it were different.

Anger is a choice, as well as a habit. It is a learned reaction to frustration, in which you behave in ways that you would rather not. In fact, severe anger is a form of insanity. You are insane whenever you are not in control of your behavior. Therefore, when you are angry and out of control, you are temporarily insane.

There is no psychological reward for anger. As defined here, anger is debilitating. In the physiological realm, it can produce hypertension, ulcers, rashes, heart palpitations, insomnia, fatigue and even heart disease. In the psychological sense, anger breaks down love relationships, interferes with communication, leads to guilt and depression and generally just gets in your way. You may be skeptical, since you've always heard that expressing your anger is healthier than keeping it bottled up inside of you. Yes, the expression of anger is indeed a healthier alternative than suppressing it. But there is an even healthier stance—not having the anger at all. In this case you won't be confronted with the dilemma of whether to let it out or keep it in.

Like all emotions, anger is the result of thinking. It is not something that simply happens to you. When faced with circumstances that are not going the way you would like them to, you tell yourself that things shouldn't be that way (frustration) and then you select a familiar angry response which serves a purpose. (See the payoff section later in this chapter.) And as long as you think of anger as a part of what it means to be a human being, you have a reason to accept it, and avoid going to work on it.

By all means give vent to your anger, let it out in nondestructive ways—if you are still deciding to have it. But begin to think of yourself as someone who can learn to think new thoughts when you are frustrated, so that the immobilizing anger can be replaced by more fulfilling emotions. Annoyance, irritation, and disappointment are feelings that you will very likely continue to experience, since the world will never be the way you want it. But anger, that hurtful emotional response to obstacles, can be eliminated.

You may make a case for anger because it works in getting your way. Well, take a closer look. If you mean that raising your voice or looking upset will help you keep your two-year-old child from playing in the street where she might get hurt, then raising your voice is an excellent strategy. It only becomes anger when you are genuinely upset, when you get flushed, and increase your heartbeat, when you slam things around and are generally immobilized for any period of time. By all means select personal strategies that will reinforce appropriate behavior, but don't take all of the internal hurt that goes with it. You can learn to think like this: "This behavior she is exhibiting is dangerous to her. I want to make her see that playing in the street will not be tolerated. I'll raise my voice to demonstrate my strong feelings about it. But I won't go around being mad."

Consider a typical mother who cannot master this controlled display of anger. She is constantly upset about her children's repetitious bad behavior. It seems that the more upset she gets, the more they misbehave. She punishes them, sends them to their room, screams constantly and is almost always in a state of pique when dealing with the kids. Her life as a mother is a battle. Loud voices are the only thing she knows, and each evening she is an emotional wreck, drained from a day on the battlefield.

So why don't the kids behave when they know how upset Mommy decides to be whenever they act up? Because the irony of anger is that it never works in changing others; it only intensifies the other person's desire to control the angry person. Listen to the above children, assuming they could give voice to their own rationale for misbehaving.

"See what it takes to set Mommy off? All you have to do is say this, or do that, and you can get control over her and send her into one of her fits. You may have to stay in your room for a short while, but look at what you get! Complete emotional domination over her for such a low price. Since we have so little power over her, let's do this some more and watch her go bananas over our behavior."

Anger, when used in any relationship, will almost always encourage the other person to continue to act as he has been. While the provoker may act scared, he also knows that he can set the other person off whenever he wants, and therefore exercise the same kind of vindictive authority as the angry individual thinks he has.

Whenever you select anger as a response to someone else's behavior, you are withholding from that person the right to be what he chooses. Inside your head is the neurotic sentence, "Why can't you be more like me? Then I would like you now, instead of being angry." But others will never be the way you want them to be, all of the time. Much of the time people and things will not go the way you would like them to go. That's the way the world is. And the likelihood of it changing is zero. So, every time you choose anger when you run into someone or something you don't like, you are deciding to be hurt or in some way immobilized because of reality. Now that's really silly. Being upset about things that aren't ever going to change. Instead of choosing anger, you can begin to think of others as having a right to be different from what you'd prefer. You may not like it, but you don't have to be angry about it. Anger will only encourage them to continue as they are, and will bring about all of the physical stress and mental torture described above. The choice is really yours. Anger or new sentences about things that will help you to eliminate the need for the anger.

Perhaps you see yourself in the opposite camp, that is, someone who has a great deal of anger, but has never had the courage to express it. You keep it in and never say a thing, building yourself up for those painful ulcers, and living with a lot of present-moment anxiety. But this is not the opposite of the individual who rants and rages. You have the same sentences in your head that people and things should be the way you want them to be. If they were, you reason, you wouldn't feel anger. This is faulty logic, and eradicating it is the secret to getting rid of your tension. While you will want to learn to express pent-up anger instead of storing it up, the ultimate goal is to learn to think in new ways that will not create the anger. Such internal thoughts as:

"If he wants to be a fool, I'm not going to choose to be upset. He, not me, owns his dumb behavior" or "Things aren't going the way I think they should. While I don't like it, I'm not going to immobilize myself."

Learning to express the anger with courageous kinds of new behaviors that have been discussed throughout this book is your first step. Then, thinking in new ways that will help you to shift from the external to the internal side of the mental health ledger, refusing to own anyone else's behavior is the ultimate step. You can learn not to give other people's behavior and ideas the power to upset you. By thinking highly of yourself and refusing to let others control you, you won't hurt yourself with present-moment anger.

Having a Sense of Humor

It is impossible for you to be angry and laugh at the same time. Anger and laughter are mutually exclusive and you have the power to choose either.

Laughter is the sunshine of the soul. And without sunshine nothing can live or grow. As Winston Churchill put it,

> It is my belief, you cannot deal with the most serious things in the world unless you understand the most amusing.

You may take life too seriously. Perhaps the single most outstanding characteristic of healthy people is their unhostile sense of humor. Helping others choose to laugh, and learning to stand back and observe the incongruity of almost every life situation is an excellent remedy for anger.

In the scheme of things, what you do and whether you are angry or not will have all the impact of another glass of water being thrown over Niagara Falls. Whether you choose laughter or anger will not matter much—

except that the former will fill your present moments with happiness, and the latter will waste them in misery.

Do you take yourself and your life so seriously that you can't stand back and view the absurdity of taking anything that solemnly? An absence of laughter is an indicator of pathology. When you tend to be overly sober about yourself and what you do, remind yourself that this is the only time you have. Why waste your present being angry when laughing feels so good.

Laughter just for the sake of laughing. It is its own justification. You don't have to have a reason to laugh. Just do it. Observe yourself and others in this nutty world, and then decide whether to carry around anger or to develop a sense of humor that will give you and others one of the most priceless gifts of all—laughter. It feels so good.

Some Common Causes of Anger

You can see anger in operation all the time. Examples of people experiencing varying degrees of immobility, from mild upset to blind rage, are everywhere. It is the cancer, albeit a learned one, that permeates human interactions. Below are some of the more common instances in which people choose anger.

• Anger in the automobile. Drivers scream at other motorists for virtually everything. Pulse-racing behavior results when someone else is going too slow, too fast, doesn't signal, signals improperly, changes lanes or any number of mistakes. As a driver, you may experience a great deal of anger and emotional immobility because of the things you tell yourself about the ways others should be driving. Similarly, traffic jams are key signals for attacks of anger and hostility. Drivers yell at passengers and swear at the cause of the delay. All this behavior is the result of a single thought, "This shouldn't be happening, and because it is, I'm going to be upset and help others to choose unhappiness as well."

• Anger in competitive games. Bridge, tennis, pinochle, poker and a variety of other games are excellent anger inducers. People get angry at partners or opponents for not doing it right or for infractions of the rules. They may throw things like a tennis racket because they made an error. While stomping and throwing equipment are healthier than hitting or screaming at others, they are still barriers to present-moment fulfillment.

• Anger at the out of place. Many people feel rage at an individual or event which they consider out of place. For example, a driver in traffic may decide the cyclist or pedestrian shouldn't be there and try to drive him off the road. This kind of anger can be extremely dangerous. Many so-called accidents are actually the result of just such incidents in which uncontrolled rage has serious results.

• Anger about taxes. No amount of anger will ever change the tax laws of our country, but people rage just the same because taxes aren't what they would like them to be.

• Anger over the tardiness of others. If you expect others to function on your timetable, you will choose anger when they do not and justify your immobilization with, "I have a right to be angry. He kept me waiting half an hour."

• Anger at the disorganization or sloppiness of others. Despite the fact that your rage will probably encourage others to continue to behave in the same manner, you may persist in choosing anger.

• Anger at inanimate objects. If you hit your shin bone or hammer your thumb, reacting with a scream can be therapeutic, but feeling real rage and doing something about it such as driving your fist through a wall is not only futile, but painful as well.

• Anger over the loss of objects. No amount of rage will turn up a lost key or wallet and will probably prevent you from launching an effective search.

• Anger over world events beyond your control. You may not approve of politics, foreign relations, or the economy, but your anger and subsequent immobilization aren't going to change anything.

The Many Faces of Anger

Now that we've seen some of the occasions on which you might choose anger, let's look at some forms anger takes.

- Being verbally abusive or ridiculing a spouse, children, or loved ones, or friends.
- Physical violence—hitting, kicking, slamming—objects or people. Carried to extremes, this behavior leads to crimes of violence which are almost always committed under the influence of immobilizing anger. Murder and assaults don't occur unless emotions are out of control and anger has led to temporary insanity. Believing that anger is normal or subscribing to the psychological schools that encourage you to get in touch with your anger and let it out can be potentially dangerous. Similarly, television, movies and books which popularize anger and violence and present them as normal undermine both the individual and society.
- Saying things like, "He infuriates me," or "You really aggravate me." In these cases you are choosing to let someone else's behavior make you unhappy.
- Using phrases like, "kill him," "clobber them," or "destroy the opposition." You may think they're only expressions, but they encourage anger and violence and make it acceptable even in friendly competition.
- Temper tantrums. Not only is this a common expression of anger, it frequently serves to get the tantrum thrower exactly what he wants.
- Sarcasm, ridicule and the silent treatment. These expressions of anger can be just as damaging as physical violence.

While the list of possible anger behavior could go on into eternity, the above examples constitute the most common incidents of anger as it surfaces in this erroneous zone.

The Reward System That You've Constructed for Choosing Anger

Getting a grip on lengthening your fuse will most effectively start with some insight into the reasons for using it in the first place. Here are some of the psychological motives for keeping that fuse as short as it is.

• Whenever you find it difficult to handle yourself, feel frustrated or defeated, you can use anger to direct the responsibility for how you feel to the person or event itself, rather than taking charge of your own feelings.

• You can use your anger to manipulate those who fear you. This is particularly effective in getting those who are younger, or physically or psychologically smaller, in line.

• Anger draws attention and thus you can feel important and powerful.

• Anger is a handy excuse. You can go insane—temporarily—and then excuse yourself by saying, "I couldn't help myself." Thus you can exonerate your behavior with out-of-control logic.

• You can get your way because others would rather placate you than have to put up with the angry exhibition.

• If you are afraid of intimacy or love, you can get angry over something, and thus avoid the risky business of sharing yourself affectionately.

• You can manipulate others with guilt by having them wonder "Where did I go wrong to make him so angry?" When they feel guilty, you are powerful.

• You can break down communication in which you feel threatened because someone else is more skillful. You simply use anger to avoid the risk of looking bad.

• You don't have to work on yourself when you are angry. Therefore you can use up your present moments in the easy business of being fierce and avoid doing whatever it might take to improve yourself. Thus you can use anger to take the heat off yourself.

• You can indulge in self-pity after you've had an attack of anger and feel sorry for yourself because nobody understands you.

• You can avoid thinking clearly, simply by getting angry. Everyone knows that you can't think straight at these times, so why not haul out the old anger when you want to avoid any of the hard straight-thinking.

• You can excuse losing or poor performance with a simple fit of temper. Maybe you can even get others to stop winning, because they fear your anger so much.

• You can excuse anger by saying you need it to help you carry out some task, but in fact anger is immobilizing and never improves performance.

• By saying it's human to be angry, you have a ready justification for yourself. "I'm human, and that's what humans do."

Some Designs for Replacing Anger

Anger can be eliminated. It will require a great deal of new thinking and it can be done only one present moment at a time. When confronted with people or events which provoke you to choose anger, become aware of what you are telling yourself, and then work at new sentences which will create new feelings and more productive behavior. Here are some specific strategies for attacking anger.

• First and most important, get in touch with your thoughts at the time of your anger, and remind yourself that you don't have to think that way, simply because you've always done so in the past. Awareness is paramount.

• Try postponing anger. If you typically react with

anger in a particular circumstance, postpone the anger for fifteen seconds, and then explode in your typical fashion. Next try thirty seconds, and keep lengthening the intervals. Once you begin to see that you can put anger off, you'll have learned control. Postponing is control, and with lots of practice, you'll eventually eliminate it totally.

• When trying to use anger constructively to teach a child something, try faking the anger. Raise your voice and look stern, but don't experience all of the physical and psychological pain that goes with anger.

• Don't try to delude yourself into believing that you enjoy something that you find distasteful. You can dislike something and still not have to be angry about it.

• Remind yourself at the moment of anger that everyone has a right to be what he chooses and that your demanding that anyone be different will simply prolong your anger. Work at allowing others to choose just as you insist on your own right to do the same.

• Ask someone that you trust to help. Have them tell you when they see your anger, either verbally or with an agreed signal. When you get the signal, think about what you're doing and then try the postponing strategy.

• Keep an anger journal, and record the exact time, place and incident in which you chose to be angry. Be religious about the entries, force yourself to record all angry behavior. You'll soon find, if you are persistent, that the very act of having to write the incident down will persuade you to choose anger less often.

• Announce after you have had an angry outburst that you've just slipped and that one of your goals is to think differently so that you don't experience this anger. The verbal announcement will put you in touch with what you've done, and will demonstrate that you are truly working on yourself.

• Try being physically close to someone that you love at the moment of your anger. One way to neutralize your hostility is to hold hands, despite your inclination not to, and keep holding hands until you've expressed how you feel and dissipated your anger.

• Talk with those who are the most frequent recipients of your anger at a time when you are not angry. Share with each other the most anger-provoking activities in the other, and devise a way of communicating your feelings without debilitating anger. Perhaps a written note, or a messenger, or a cooling-off walk can be mutually agreed upon, so that you don't continue abusing each other with senseless anger. After several cooling-off walks, you'll begin to see the folly of striking out.

• Defuse your anger for the first few seconds by labeling how you feel, and how you believe your partner feels as well. The first ten seconds are the most crucial. Once you've passed these, your anger will often have subsided.

• Keep in mind all the things you believe will be met with disapproval by fifty percent of the folks, fifty percent of the time. Once you expect others to disagree, you will not choose to feel angry. Instead, you'll say to yourself that the world is straight since people aren't agreeing with everything I say, think, feel and do.

• Keep in mind that while the expression of anger is a healthy alternative to storing it up, not having it at all is the healthiest choice of all. Once you stop viewing anger as natural or only human, you'll have an internal rationale for going to work at eliminating it.

• Get rid of the expectations you have for others. When the expectations go away, so will the anger.

• Remind yourself that children will always be active and loud and getting angry about it won't do any good. While you can help children to make constructive choices in other areas, you will never be able to alter their basic nature.

• Love yourself. If you do, you won't ever burden yourself with that self-destructive anger.

• In a traffic jam, time yourself. See how long you can go without exploding. Work at the control aspect. Instead of hollering at a passenger, ask him a civil

question. Use the time creatively to write a letter, or a
song, or to devise ways out of the traffic jam, or relive
the most exciting sexual experience of your life, or
better yet, plan to improve on it.

• Instead of being an emotional slave to every frustrating circumstance, use the situation as a challenge
to change it, and you'll have no present moment time
for the anger.

Anger gets in the way. It is good for nothing. Like
all erroneous zones, anger is a means of using things
outside yourself to explain how you feel. Forget others.
Make your own choices—and don't let them be angry
ones.

XII
Portrait of a Person Who Has Eliminated All Erroneous Zones

> They are too busy *being* to notice what their neighbors are doing.

The person who is devoid of all erroneous zone behavior may seem to be a fictional character, but being free from self-destructive behavior is not a mythological concept; rather it's a real possibility. Being fully functioning is within your grasp and complete present-moment mental health can be a choice. This final chapter is devoted to a description of how people who are free from all erroneous zone thinking and behavior function. You will see the development of an individual who is unlike the majority of people, and distinguishable by an uncanny ability to be creatively alive at every moment.

People free from erroneous zones are different from run-of-the-mill individuals. While they look very much like everyone else, they possess distinct qualities, none of which are racial, socioeconomic, or sexual. They do not fit neatly into any roles, job descriptions, geographic patterns, educational levels or financial statistics. There is a different quality about them, but the difference is not discernible in the traditional external factors by which we generally classify people. They may be rich or poor, male or female, black or white, living anywhere, and doing just about anything. They are a varied group and yet they share a single trait, freedom from erroneous zones. How can you tell when you run into someone like this? Watch them! Listen to them! This is what you'll discover.

First and most obviously, you see people who like virtually everything about life—people who are comfortable doing just about anything, and who waste no time in complaining, or wishing that things were otherwise. They are enthusiastic about life, and they want all that they can get out of it. They like picnics, movies, books, sports, concerts, cities, farms, animals, mountains and just about everything. They like life. When you are around people like this you'll note an absence of grumbling, moaning, or even passive sighing. If it rains, they like it. If it's hot, they dig it, rather than complain about it. If they are in a traffic jam, or at a party, or all alone, they simply deal with what is there. There is no pretending to enjoy, but a sensible acceptance of what is, and an outlandish ability to delight in that reality. Ask them what they don't like and they are hard pressed to come up with an honest answer. They don't have sense enough to come in out of the rain, because they see rain as beautiful, thrilling and something to experience. They like it. Slush doesn't send them into a fury; they observe it, splash around in it, and accept it as part of what it means to be alive. Do they like cats? Yes. Bears? Yes. Worms? Yes. While such annoyances as disease, droughts, mosquitoes, floods and the like are not warmly embraced by such people, they never spend any of their present moments complaining about them, or wishing that they weren't so. If situations need to be eradicated, they will work at eradicating them—and enjoy the work. Try as you might, you'll have a tough time coming up with something they'll dislike doing. Truly they are likers of life, and they wallow in all of it, getting out of it all that is possible for them.

Healthy fulfilled people are free from guilt and all

the attendant anxiety that goes with using any present moments in being immobilized over past events. Certainly they can admit to making mistakes, and they can vow to avoid repeating certain behavior that is counterproductive in any way, but they do not waste their time wishing that they hadn't done something, or being upset because they dislike something that they did at an earlier moment in life. Complete freedom from guilt is one hallmark of healthy individuals. No lamenting the past and no efforts to make others choose guilt by asking such inane questions as, "Why didn't you do it differently?" or "Aren't you ashamed of yourself?" They seem to recognize that life lived through is just that, and no amount of feeling bad will alter the past. They are free from guilt themselves without any effort; because it is natural, they never help others to choose guilt. They see that feeling bad in the present moment only reinforces a poor self-image, and that learning from the past is far superior to remonstrating about the past. You'll never see them manipulating others by telling them how bad they've been, nor will you be able to manipulate them with the same tactics. They won't get angry at you, they'll simply ignore you. Rather than being upset with you, they'll go away, or change the subject. The strategies that work so beautifully on most people fail with these healthy individuals. Rather than make themselves and others miserable with guilt, they unceremoniously pass when it comes along.

Similarly, people free of erroneous zones are nonworriers. Circumstances that drive many people to frenzy barely affect these individuals. They are neither planners nor putters-away for the future. They refuse to worry and they keep themselves free from the anxiety that accompanies worry. They don't know how to worry. It is not a part of their makeup. They are not necessarily calm at all moments, but they are unwilling to spend present moments agonizing about things in the future over which they have no control. They are very present-moment oriented, and they have an internal signal that seems to remind them that all worrying must take place in the present moment, and that it is a foolish way to go about living one's current life.

These people live now, rather than in the past or the future. They are not threatened by the unknown, and they seek out experiences that are new and unfamiliar to them. They love ambiguity. They savor the now at all times, aware that this is all they have. They don't plan for a future event and let long periods of inactivity elapse as they await that event. The moments between events are just as livable as those taken up by the events themselves, and they have an uncanny ability to get every pleasure out of their daily lives. They are not postponers, saving for a rainy day, and while our culture disapproves their behavior, they are unthreatened by self-reproach. They gather in their happiness now, and when a future now arrives, they gather in that one as well. These individuals are always enjoying simply because they see the folly of waiting to enjoy. It is a natural way of living, very much like that of a child or an animal. They are busy grabbing present-moment fulfillment, while most people spend their lives waiting for payoffs, and never being able to seize them.

These healthy people are strikingly independent. They are out of the nest, and while they may have a strong love for and devotion to family, they see independence as superior to dependence in all relationships. They treasure their own freedom from expectations. Their relationships are built upon mutual respect for the right of an individual to make decisions for himself. Their love involves no imposition of values on the loved one. They put a high premium on privacy, which may leave others feeling snubbed or rejected. They like to be alone at times, and they will go to great lengths to ensure that their privacy is protected. You will not find these people involved in numerous love relationships. They are selective about their love, but they're also deeply and sensitively loving. It is difficult for dependent or unhealthy people to love them, because they are adamant about their freedom. If someone needs them, they reject such a need as hurtful to the other person as well as to themselves. They want those they love to be independent, to make their own choices, and to live their lives for themselves. While they enjoy others and want to be with them, they want even more for others to make it without crutches or leaning. Thus, the moment you start leaning on these people, you'll find them disappearing, first emotionally, and then physically as well. They refuse to be dependent, or depended upon, in a mature relationship. With children, they provide a model of a caring person, but they encourage self-reliance almost from the very beginning with a great amount of love offered at every turn.

You will find an uncommon absence of approval-seeking in these happy, fulfilled individuals. They are able to function without approval and applause from others. They do not seek out honors as most people do. They are unusually free from the opinion of others, almost uncaring about whether someone else likes what they've said or done. They do not attempt to shock others, or to gain their approval. These are people who are so internally directed that they are literally unconcerned about others' evaluations of their behavior. They are not oblivious to applause and approval; they just don't seem to need it. They can be almost blunt in their honesty since they do not couch their messages in carefully worded phrases designed to please. If you want to know what they think, that is exactly what you'll hear. Conversely, when you say something about them they will not be destroyed or immobilized. They will take the data you provide, filter it through their own values and use it for growth. They do not need to be loved by everyone, nor do they harbor the inordinate wish to be approved by all for everything that they do. They recognize that they will always incur some disapproval. They are unusual in that they are able to function as they, rather than some external other, dictates.

As you watch these characters you will note a lack of enculturation. They are not rebels, but they do make their own choices even if those choices conflict with what everybody else does. They can ignore petty rules if they make no sense, and quietly shrug at the little conventions that are such an important part of so many lives. They're not cocktail partiers, nor do they engage in small talk because it's the polite thing to do. They are their own people and while they see society as an important part of their lives, they refuse to be ruled by it or to become a slave to it. They don't rebelliously attack but they do know internally when to ignore and function in a clear-headed and sensible way.

They know how to laugh, and how to create laughter. They find humor in virtually all situations, and they can laugh at the most absurd as well as the most solemn of occasions. They love to help others to laugh, and they are facile at creating humor. These are not serious, ponderous folks who plow through life with a stony grimness. Instead, they are doers, who are often scorned for being frivolous at the wrong time. They do not have good timing for they know that there is really no such thing as the right thing in the right place. They love the incongruous, yet they are unhostile in their humor; never, but never using ridicule to create laughter. They don't laugh at people, they laugh with them. They do laugh at life, and they see the whole thing as fun, even though they are deliberate in their own pursuits. When they step back and look at life, they know that they aren't going any place in particular, and they are able to enjoy and create an atmosphere in which others can choose joy for themselves. They are fun to have around.

These are people who accept themselves without complaint. They know that they are human beings, and that being so involves certain human attributes. They know that they look a certain way, and they accept it. If they're tall, that's okay, but so is being short. Bald is fine, and so is lots of hair. They can live with sweat! They are not phony about their physical humanity. They've accepted themselves, and therefore they are the most natural of people. No hiding behind artificialities, no apologizing for what they are. They don't know how to be offended by anything that is human. They like themselves and accept what they are. Similarly, they accept all of nature for what it is, rather than wishing it were otherwise. They never complain about things that won't change, such as heat waves, rainstorms, or cold water. They accept themselves and the world as it is. No pretenses, no groaning, simply acceptance. Follow them around for years, and you'll never hear self-deprecation or wishing. You'll see doers doing. You'll see them observing the world the way it is, like a child who accepts the natural world and enjoys it for all it's worth.

They appreciate the natural world. They love being outdoors in nature, and tripping around in all that is unspoiled and original. They especially love things like mountains, sunsets, rivers, flowers, trees, animals and virtually all flora and fauna. They are naturalists as people, unceremonious and unpretentious, and they love the naturalness of the universe. They are not busy seeking out taverns, night clubs, parties, conventions, smoke-filled rooms, and the like, although they are certainly capable of enjoying such activities to the fullest. They are at peace with nature, God's world, if you will, though they are capable of functioning in a man-made world. They are also capable of appreciating what has become stale for others. They never tire of a sunset or a trip in the woods. A bird in flight is a magnificent sight over and over again. A caterpillar never grows tiresome, nor does a cat giving birth to kittens. Over and over again they spontaneously appreciate. Some may find this artificial, but these people don't notice what others think. They are too busy in awe of the vastness of possibilities for present-moment fulfillment.

They have insight into the behavior of others, and what may seem complex and indecipherable to others, they see as clear and understandable. The problems that immobilize so many others are often viewed as only minor annoyances by these people. This lack of emotional involvement in problems makes them able to surmount barriers that remain insurmountable to others.

They have insight into themselves too, and they recognize immediately what others are attempting to do to them. They can shrug and ignore while others are angered and immobilized. They are never perplexed or stumped and what may seem to be confusing or insoluble to most others is often viewed by them as a simple condition with a ready resolution. They are not focused on problems in their emotional world. For these people a problem is really only an obstacle to be overcome rather than a reflection of what they are or aren't as a person. Their self-worth is located within, and therefore any external concerns can be viewed objectively, rather than as in any way a threat to their value. This is a most difficult trait to understand, since most people are easily threatened by external events, ideas, or people. But healthy, independent people do not know how to be threatened, and this very characteristic may make them threatening to others.

They never engage in useless fighting. They are not bandwagoners, jumping on various causes as a way of bringing importance to themselves. If fighting will help bring about change, then they will fight but never will they find it necessary to fight uselessly. They are not martyrs. They are doers. They are also helpers. They are almost always engaged in work that will make other people's lives more pleasant or tolerable. They are warriors on the forefront of social change, and yet they don't take their struggles to bed with them every night as a breeding ground for ulcers, heart disease and other physical disorders. They are incapable of stereotyping. They often don't even notice the physical differences in people, including racial, ethnic, size and sexual. They are not surface people, judging others by their looks. While they may appear to be hedonistic and selfish, they spend vast amounts of time in the service of others. Why? Because they like it that way.

These are not sickly people. They don't believe in being immobilized by colds and headaches. They believe in their ability to rid themselves of such maladies, and they never go around telling others how bad they feel, how tired they are, or what diseases are currently infecting their bodies. They treat their bodies well. They like themselves, and consequently they eat well, exercise regularly (as a way of living) and refuse to experience most of the infirmities that render many people helpless for various periods of time. They like to live well, and they do.

Another hallmark of these fully functioning individuals is honesty. They are not evasive with their responses, nor do they pretend or lie about anything. They see lying as a distortion of their own reality, and they will not participate in self-delusional behavior. While they are private people they will also avoid having to distort to protect others. They know that they are in charge of their own world, and that others are as well. Thus, they will behave in ways that will often be perceived as cruel but in fact they are simply allowing others to make their own decisions. They deal effectively with what is, rather than what they would like to be.

These people don't blame. They are internal in their personality orientation, and they refuse to ascribe responsibility to others for what they are. Similarly, they will not spend a great deal of time talking about others and focusing on what someone else has done or failed to do. They do not talk about people, they talk with them. They do not blame others, they help others and themselves to assign responsibility where it belongs. They are not gossips or spreaders of evil information. They are so busy being effective in their own lives that they have no time for the petty connivances that occupy many people's lives. Doers do. Critics blame and complain.

These individuals have little concern with order, organization, or systems in their lives. They have self-discipline but no need to have things and people fit into their own perceptions of how everything ought to be. They have no oughts for others. They see everyone as having choices, and those petty things that drive others insane are simply the results of someone else's decision. They do not see the world as having to be any special way. They have no preoccupation with cleanliness or orderliness. They exist in a functional way, and if everything isn't fitting in as they would prefer, they find that all right too. Organization then, for these people, is simply a useful means rather than an end in itself. Because of this lack of organizational neurosis, they are creative. They attack any concern in their own unique way, be it making a bowl of soup, writing a report, or mowing the grass. They apply their own imagination to the act, and the result is a creative approach to everything. They don't have to do it a certain way. They don't consult manuals or ask experts; they simply attack the problem as they see fit. This is creativity, and without exception, they have it.

These are people with exceptionally high energy levels. They seem to require less sleep, and yet they are excited about living. They do, and they are healthy. They can muster tremendous surges of energy for completing a task because they choose to be involved in it as a fulfilling present-moment activity. Their energy is not supernatural; it is simply the result of loving life and all the activities in it. They don't know how to be bored. All life events present opportunities for doing, thinking, feeling and living, and they know how to apply their energy in virtually all life circumstances. Were they to be imprisoned, they would use their minds in creative ways to avoid the paralysis of loss of interest. Boredom is not in their lives because they are channeling the same energy that others have in ways productive for themselves.

They are aggressively curious. They never know enough. They search for more and want to learn each and every present moment of their lives. They are not concerned with having to do it right or having done it wrong. If it doesn't work, or it doesn't accomplish the greatest amount of good, then it is discarded, rather than mulled over in regret. They are truth seekers in the learning sense, always excited about learning more and never believing they are a finished product. If they are around a barber, they want to learn about barbering. They never feel or act superior, showing off their merit badges for others to applaud. They learn from children and stockbrokers and animals. They want to know more about what it means to be a welder, a cook, a hooker, or a corporate vice-president. They are learners not teachers. They never know enough, and they don't know how to act snobbish or superior, since they never feel that way. Every person, every object, every event represents an opportunity for knowing more. And they are aggressive in their interests, not waiting for information to come along, but going after it. They're not afraid to talk to a waitress, ask a dentist what it feels like to have your hands in someone's mouth all day, or inquire of the poet what is meant by this or that line.

They are not afraid to fail. In fact, they often welcome it. They do not equate being successful in any enterprise with being successful as a human being. Since their self-worth comes from within, any external event can be viewed objectively as simply effective or ineffective. They know that failing is merely somebody else's editorial opinion and not to be feared since it cannot affect self-worth. Thus, they will try anything, participate just because it's fun, and never fear having to explain themselves. Similarly, they never choose anger in any immobilizing way. Using the same logic (and not having to think it through each time since it has become a way of life) they don't say to themselves that other people should behave differently and that events should be otherwise. They accept others as they are, and they work at changing events that they dislike. Thus, anger is impossible because the expectancies are not there. These are people who are capable of eliminating emotions that are in any way self-destructive and facilitating those which are self-enhancing.

These happy individuals display an admirable lack

of defensiveness. They won't play games and try to impress others. They don't dress for others' approval, nor do they go through the motions of explaining themselves. They have a simplicity and naturalness, and they won't get seduced into making issues of small or big things. They aren't arguers or hot-headed debaters; they simply state their views, listen to others and recognize the futility of trying to convince someone else to be as they are. They'll simply say, "That's all right; we're just different. We don't have to agree." They let it go at that without any need to win an argument or persuade the opponent of the wrongness of his position. They are unafraid of giving a bad impression but they don't strive to do so.

Their values are not local. They do not identify with the family, neighborhood, community, city, state, or country. They see themselves as belonging to the human race, and an unemployed Austrian is no better or worse than an unemployed Californian. They are not patriotic to a special boundary; rather they see themselves as a part of the whole of humanity. They take no glee in having more enemy dead, since the enemy is as human as the ally. The lines drawn by men to describe how one should be affiliated are not subscribed to. They transcend traditional boundaries, which often causes others to label them as rebels or even traitors.

They have no heroes or idols. They view all people as human, and they place no one above themselves in importance. They do not demand justice at every turn. When someone else has more privileges, they see that as a benefit to that person, rather than as a reason for being unhappy. When playing an opponent they want him to do well, rather than wishing a poor performance in order to win by default. They want to be victorious and effective on their own, rather than gaining through the shortcomings of others. They do not insist that everyone be equally endowed, but look inward for their happiness. They are not critics, nor do they take pleasure in other people's misfortunes. They are too busy being, to notice what their neighbors are doing.

Most significantly, these are individuals who love themselves. They are motivated by a desire to grow, and they always treat themselves well when given the option. They have no room for self-pity, self-rejection, or self-hate. If you ask them, "Do you like yourself?" you'll get a resounding, "Of course I do!" They are rare birds indeed. Each day is a delight. They have it together and they live all of their present moments. They are not problem free, but free from emotional immobility as a result of the problems. The measure of their mental health is not in whether they slip but in what they do when they slip. Do they lie there and whine about having fallen? No, they get up, dust themselves off, and get on with the business of living. People who are free from erroneous zones don't chase after happiness; they live and happiness is their payoff.

This quote from a *Reader's Digest* piece on happiness sums up the approach to effective living that we've been talking about.

Nothing on earth renders happiness less approachable than trying to find it. Historian Will Durant described how he looked for happiness in knowledge, and found only disillusionment. He then sought happiness in travel and found weariness; in wealth and found discord and worry. He looked for happiness in his writing and was only fatigued. One day he saw a woman waiting in a tiny car with a sleeping child in her arms. A man descended from a train and came over and gently kissed the woman and then the baby, very softly so as not to waken him. The family drove off and left Durant with a stunning realization of the real nature of happiness. He relaxed and discovered that "every normal function of life holds some delight."*

By using your own present moments for maximizing

* "The One Sure Way to Happiness" by June Callwood, October 1974.

fulfillment, you'll be one of these people rather than an observer. It's such a delightful idea—freedom from erroneous zones. You can make that choice right now—if you choose to!

Index

HOW TO MANAGE YOUR BOSS

Derek Rowntree

THE COMPLETE GUIDE TO CONTROLLING YOUR DESTINY AT WORK

The most common cause of complaint at work is 'The Boss': the power-hungry boss, the boss who exploits, the boss who overlooks, the incompetant boss, and the boss who simply shouldn't be a boss at all. In all cases they are unlikely to change, but they can be *influenced* – by YOU.

How To Manage Your Boss is a step-by-step guide over the hurdles of working life. It takes you through the sensitive issues of criticism, trust, assertiveness, power and dependency, of how to claim your successes and admit your failures, and shows you the way to the ultimate goal – improving your job.

MANAGEMENT
0 7474 0052

PUTTNAM

Andrew Yule

In 1986 David Puttnam – the 'blitz baby' from London – was lured to Hollywood to transform one of the most powerful film corporations in the world. One year later his relationship with Columbia Pictures was abruptly terminated. Britain's most famous movie mogul left Tinseltown – taking a massive payoff and leaving a lot of unanswered questions.

Drawing on extensive interviews with his family, friends, foes and colleagues, and with David Puttnam himself, Andrew Yule presents a frank, unflinching and glittering portrait of a man who rose from the advertising world of the Swinging Sixties to become one of the foremost movie-makers of the century. From the controversial *Midnight Express* to the glorious *Chariots of Fire*, from the horror of *The Killing Fields* to the inspiration of *The Mission*, he shows how the dreams of David Puttnam captivated millions. And how they led to a Hollywood disaster that wasn't a movie . . .

BIOGRAPHY
0 7474 0107 1

Sphere now offers an exciting range of quality fiction and non-fiction by both established and new authors. All of the books in this series are available from good bookshops, or can be ordered from the following address:

Sphere Books
Cash Sales Department
P.O. Box 11
Falmouth
Cornwall TR10 9EN.

Please send cheque or postal order (no currency), and allow 60p for postage and packing for the first book plus 25p for the second book and 15p for each additional book ordered up to a maximum charge of £1.90 in U.K.

B.F.P.O. customers please allow 60p for the first book, 25p for the second book plus 15p per copy for the next 7 books, thereafter 9p per book.

Overseas customers including Eire please allow £1.25 for postage and packing for the first book, 75p for the second book and 28p for each subsequent title ordered.